NOTES ON
THE HEBREW TEXT OF I KINGS
XVII–XIX AND XXI–XXII

NOTES ON THE

HEBREW TEXT OF I KINGS

XVII–XIX AND XXI–XXII

by

NORMAN H. SNAITH

M.A., D.D.(Oxon), Hon. D.D.(Glasg.)

*Tutor in Old Testament Languages and Literature
at Wesley College, Headingley, Leeds*

LONDON

THE EPWORTH PRESS

THE EPWORTH PRESS
(FRANK H. CUMBERS)

25-35 City Road, London, E.C.1

MELBOURNE   CAPE TOWN
NEW YORK   TORONTO

MADE AND PRINTED IN GREAT BRITAIN BY PURNELL AND SONS, LTD.
PAULTON (SOMERSET) AND LONDON

PREFACE

THESE notes are designed particularly for beginners who may be studying these chapters as their first Hebrew text. Especially are they designed for students whose circumstances compel them to study by themselves, without being in touch with anyone who can guide them in regular tuition. References are given, wherever necessary, to the relevant pages in Davidson's *Introductory Hebrew Grammar*, twentieth and later editions (DG), and to Wood and Lanchester's *A Hebrew Grammar* (WL), these being the grammars most used by elementary students. Further references are given to Davidson's *Hebrew Syntax* (DS), Gesenius-Kautzsch's *Hebrew Grammar*, the second English edition, translated by A. E. Cowley (GK, by paragraphs), and to Driver's *Hebrew Tenses* (DT). The reference BDB is to the *Oxford Hebrew Lexicon* by Brown, Driver and Briggs.

I am greatly indebted to Mr. Eric Powell, M.A., B.D., of Woodhouse Grove School, near Bradford, for very considerable help in checking both the manuscript and the proofs. We have taken every care to ensure complete accuracy, and we hope we have succeeded.

N. H. S.

CHAPTER XVII

Verse 1. וַיֹּאמֶר. Strong-*waw* (*waw*-consecutive, *waw*-conversive, DG 84f, WL 88–91, DS 70–78, DT 70–99, GK 49*a–g* and 111*a–x*) plus 3 m. s. impf. qal of אמר (say). The accent of the 3 m. s. impf. is normally on the last syllable, but, when the previous syllable is open, the tone is retracted with strong-*waw* (DG 85f, WL 90, DT 74, GK 49*d*) unless the word itself is in pause at the end of the phrase. Here, the final vowel, normally *pathach*, becomes *seghol*, DG 119, WL 172 (note 2). The root is one of five *pe-aleph* verbs, the mnemonic being: 'The bridegroom said אמר to the bride, I am willing אבה to eat אכל all you bake אפה though I perish אבד.'

הַתִּשְׁבִּי. Article plus תִּשְׁבִּי (Tishbite). The ending is characteristic of tribal names, DG 56, GK 86*h*.

מִתֹּשָׁבֵי. Prep. *min* (from, DG 51) plus cstr. pl. of תּוֹשָׁב (settler). The retention of the *qamets* is unusual in a pl. cstr., but see GK 93*pp*. Most scholars follow LXX and read מִתִּשְׁבֶּה (from Tishbe of).

חַי יהוה. Lit. 'JHVH is living', the common form of oath. חַי is an adjective (m.s.). יהוה is the Personal Name of God, read by the Jews as אֲדֹנָי (Adonai), represented by LORD in English Versions. The word 'Jehovah' arises from reading the consonants of the Sacred Name with the vowels (as printed) of its substitute.

7

אלהי. Cstr. of אֱלֹהִים (God), a plural form denoting majesty, GK 124g, DS 18. This is the general Hebrew word for God (gods), used in the E-source of the Pentateuch until the Personal Name is revealed at the Bush, Exod. 3¹⁴.

אשר. This word is a relative, but not a pronoun, DG 47, WL 38. In cases where the subject of the verb is a 3rd person pronoun (e.g. he, she, they), the word can be translated 'who', but the subject should be regarded as being contained in the verb and not in the relative. Here the relative is combined with the following לפניו to mean 'before whom', lit. 'wh . . . before him'.

עמדתי. 1 s. pf. qal of עמד (stand), normal form.

לפניו. Prep. lamedh plus 3 m. s. suffix to פָּנִים (faces). The ordinary Hebrew for 'before' is לִפְנֵי (DG 69, WL 65), and so here 'before him'.

אם introduces the substance of the oath. We have to insert a negative in translating, on the analogy 'I'll be cursed if I do', which means that I do not intend to do it, whereas 'I'll be cursed if I don't' means that I do intend to do it. For this latter case, Hebrew has אִם לֹא, DG 168, WL 201f, GK 149d, DS 165.

יהיה. 3 m. s. impf. qal of היה (become, be). This root and the similar root חיה (live) have some irregularities (DG 147, WL 145). With lamedh-he verbs generally, the last vowel of the 3 m. s. pf. is qamets, of the 3 m. s. impf. it is seghol, of the 2 m. s. imperat. it is tsere. The construct infinitives all end in -oth, the participles in seghol. The infinitive absolutes follow the

8

general rule for all verbs: the three on the right of the paradigms (hophal, hiphil, hithpael) have *tsere* for their last vowel, the piel has either *tsere* or -*o*, the rest have -*o*.

הָשׁנים. Article plus pl. of fem. noun שָׁנָה (year). The plural is usually in -*im*, but forms in -*oth* are also found (9 times, poetic or late).

הָאלה. Article (always with *qamets* before *resh* and *aleph*, DG 44, WL 27) plus אֵלֶּה, demonstrative (these), DG 46, WL 35.

וּמטר. *Waw*-copula plus מָטָר (rain, downpour). The vowel is -*u* before labials (b-u-m-p) and vocal *shewa*, DG 53, WL 44.

כי אם following a negative, actual or implied (as here), is 'except, but', DG 168, GK 163*a*, DS 203.

לפי. Prep. *lamedh* plus פִּי, cstr. sing. of פֶּה (mouth), DG 153, WL 186.

דברי. 1 s. suffix to singular דָּבָר (word).

Verse 2. ויהי. Strong-*waw* plus 3 m. s. impf. (apoc.) qal of היה (to be). The normal 3 m. s. impf. qal is יִהְיֶה, DG 147f, WL 145 and 20. The *dagesh-forte* fails in *yodh*-with-vocal-*shewa*, DG 32, WL 20 and 90 (3), GK 20*m*.

דבר. Cstr. sing. of דָּבָר (word).

אליו. Prep. אֶל (to) plus 3 m. s. suffix. This preposition appears to take plural suffixes, DG 70, WL 64f.

9

לאמר. Prep. *lamedh* plus inf. cstr. qal of אמר (say). Note that the vowel is *tsere* (an exception), DG 51, WL 44 (note), lit. 'to say'.

Verse 3. לֵךְ. 2 m. s. imperat. qal of הלך (go). One of six *pe-waw* verbs which have impf. qal like יֵשֵׁב. The six are: 'When she knew ידע that her daughter had borne a child ילד, she went out יצא of her house, went down ירד the steps, went הלך to her, and sat ישׁב with her.'

מזה. Prep. *min* (from) plus 3 m. s. demonstrative זֶה (this), and so 'from here'.

ופנית. Strong-*waw* (-*u* before labial, b-u-m-p, DG 53, WL 44) plus 2 m. s. pf. qal of פנה (turn), normal *lamedh-he* form. This word and the next are omitted in LXX.

לְךָ. Prep. *lamedh* plus 2 m. s. suffix, DG 51, WL 49. This idiomatic use of *lamedh* corresponds to the classical ethic dative, WL 207, DS 140. Note the *dagesh* in the *lamedh*. This is known as *dagesh forte conjunctivum*, DG 33, WL 21, GK 20f. It follows a toneless -*a*, and secures proper pronunciation of the consonant. The inseparable prepositions and the copula do not usually take this special *dagesh*, but לְךָ always does after a toneless -*a*.

קדמה. The toneless *he* (*he-locale*) is a relic of an old accusative and expresses 'direction towards', DG 61f, WL 55 and 211. Here it is added to קֶדֶם (east), and so means 'eastwards'.

ונסתרת. Strong-*waw* plus 2 m. s. pf. niphal of סתר (hide). The tone is thrown forward from the last-but-one to the last syllable, DG 85f, WL 90 (note 2).

בנחל. Prep. *beth* (in) plus cstr. sing. of נַחַל (wady), the cstr. sing. form being the same as the absolute (second declension).

על־פני. Prep. עַל (upon, against) plus cstr. of פָּנִים (lit. faces). The phrase here means 'on the east'. The Hebrews named the points of the compass by first turning towards the rising sun. South is 'right' and West is 'behind'.

הירדן. Note the article. It is always 'the Jordan', 'the Carmel', 'the Lebanon', DS 26, GK 126*e*.

Verse 4. והיה. Strong-*waw* plus 3 m. s. pf. qal of היה (be); here 'and it shall be'.

מהנחל. Prep. *min* (*tsere* before *he*, DG 52, WL 20) plus article plus נַחַל (wady).

תשתה. 2 m. s. impf. qal of שתה (drink): *seghol* in *lamedh-he* imperfect (see note on verse 2).

ואת־הערבים. The hyphen is called *maqqeph* (binder, DG 40, WL 28), and it has the effect of making the whole phrase one word. Hence אֶת, the sign of the definite accusative (DG 49, WL 28), now becomes a closed syllable before the tone and must take a short vowel (*seghol*). After the *maqqeph*, we have the article (*qamets* before ordinary *ayin*) plus plural of 3rd declension noun עֹרֵב (raven).

צויתי. 1 s. pf. piel of צוה (command), verb found only in piel and pual. The middle vowel of all the 1st s. perfects of *lamedh-he* verbs is usually *tsere*, in order to avoid three consecutive -*is*, DG 229 (bottom), WL 143.

Otherwise the passive perfects have *tsere* throughout (but not 1 pl. pf. niphal), and the actives have *chireq* throughout. In this particular root, however, the 1st s. pf. piel has *chireq* 30 times against *tsere* 5 times.

לכלכלך. Prep. *lamedh* plus inf. cstr. pilpel of כּוּל (contain) plus 2 m. s. suffix. The pilpel of this verb usually means 'sustain, nourish'. Intensive forms of *ayin-waw* (and also double-*ayin*) verbs have variant methods of doubling the middle consonant, because of the difficulty of it being a *waw*, or (for double-*ayin* verbs) of it being already found twice, DG 132, WL 160. The seghol under the second *kaph* is half-open. Verbal suffixes follow the pattern of the nouns, i.e. if the verbal form ends in -*e* or -*o*, the vowel changes follow the pattern of third declension nouns. Otherwise the changes follow the first declension.

שׁם. Adverb of place, 'there'.

Verse 5. וילך. Strong-*waw* plus 3 m. s. impf. qal of הלך (go), with tone retracted on to open syllable in the pretone (DG 85, WL 90) and last vowel shortened from the normal *tsere* to *seghol* (DG 128, WL 137). One of the six verbs having impf. qal like יֵשֵׁב (see note on verse 3).

ויעש. Strong-*waw* plus 3 m. s. impf. qal (apoc.) of עשׂה (do), DG 147, WL 144, with *pathach*s in consequence of the *pe*-guttural.

כדבר. Prep. *kaph* (half-open -*i* before vocal *shewa*, DG 50f, WL 43) plus cstr. sing. of דְּבָר (word).

וישׁב. Strong-*waw* plus 3 m. s. impf. qal of ישׁב (dwell, sit), one of the six *pe-yodh* verbs (see note on verse

12

3); tone retracted (see note above, beginning of verse 5).

Verse 6. מְבִיאִים. m. pl. hiphil ptc. מֵבִיא of בּוֹא (come): 'kept bringing'. The participle is used of continuous action, DG 159, WL 107, DS 134, GK 46*p*, DT 167.

לוֹ. Prep. *lamedh* plus 3 m. s. suffix, DG 51, WL 49.

וּבָשָׂר. *Waw*-copula (-*u* before labial, b-u-m-p, DG 53, WL 44) plus masc. noun בָּשָׂר (flesh). This word is omitted here in LXX (Vaticanus) and Lucian, just as ולחם (and bread) is omitted by them in the next clause: thus they make the ravens bring bread in the morning and flesh in the evening.

בבקר. Prep. *beth* plus article plus segholate noun בֹּקֶר (morning). The word properly means the point of time when the light 'cleaves' the darkness. Cf. בָּקָר (ox, cattle) is the animal that 'cleaves' (ploughs) the soil.

בערב. Prep. *beth* plus article plus עֶרֶב (evening) with *qamets* for the normal *seghol* in pause with *athnach*, DG 40, WL 117. The vowel here under the *beth* follows the regular rule for the article (*he* omitted) before *ayin*-with-*qamets*-and-accent, and is *qamets*, DG 44, WL 27. Properly ערב is the time when the light turns to darkness.

וּמן־הנחל. *Waw*-copula (-*u* before labial) plus *min* (from) plus *maqqeph*, etc., an alternative form for וּמהנחל (verse 4), DG 52, WL 32.

ישתה. 3 m. s. impf. qal of שתה (drink); a true imperfect, 'he was accustomed to drink'. LXX adds ὕδωρ 'water', unnecessarily.

13

Verse 7. וַיְהִי. Strong-*waw* plus 3 m. s. impf. qal (apoc.) of הָיָה (become, come to be). The accent here is dis-junctive (i.e. disconnecting with what follows, as against 'conjunctive'), DG 230f, WL 116, and the meaning is 'and it came to pass', cf. the Greek καὶ ἐγένετο. For apocopation of *lamedh-he* verbs generally, cf. DG 147, WL 144; of this verb and its parallel חיה (live), DG 147f, WL 145.

מִקֵּץ. Prep. *min* plus cstr. sing. of קֵץ (end), same form as absolute.

יָמִים. Pl. of יוֹם (day), DG 153, WL 186. The whole phrase is lit. 'from the end of days'. It usually means 'at the end of a year', but probably not in this case.

וַיִּיבַשׁ. Strong-*waw* plus 3 m. s. impf. qal of יָבֵשׁ (to be dry), an ordinary *pe-yodh* verb (though a stative with qal pf. in *tsere*) with *yodh* showing in impf. qal and *waw* in the hiphil.

הַנַּחַל. Article plus נַחַל (wady) with *qamets* for normal *pathach* in pause with *athnach*, DG 40, WL 117.

גֶשֶׁם usually refers to the seasonal rains, the 'massive, bulky' autumnal rains.

בָּאָרֶץ. Prep. *beth* plus article (*he* displaced) plus אֶרֶץ (earth). Note that the form with the article is הָאָרֶץ. DG 46, WL 27.

Verse 9. קוּם. 2 m. s. imperat. qal of קוּם (rise). These *ayin-waw* and *ayin-yodh* verbs are always quoted by the inf. cstr. qal because the vowel of the imperfect (and consequently imperative and inf. cstr. qal) is thus given.

14

צרפתה. The toneless *he* is the *he-locale* of 'direction towards', see note on verse 3. The place name is צָרְפַת in Hebrew, and Σαρεπτα in Greek.

וישבת. Strong-*waw* plus 2 m. s. pf. qal of ישב (dwell) with tone thrown forward to the last syllable according to custom, DG 85f, WL 90.

הנה. Demonstrative particle 'behold'. For suffixes, see DG 142 (note), WL 110f, GK 100*o* and (for syntax) GK 147*o*.

צויתי. See note on verse 4.

אשה אלמנה. Lit. 'a woman, a widow', where we would say 'a widow woman'. Hebrew places the wider group first, and then limits it as may be necessary, either with adjectives (and adverb) or with nouns in apposition, DS 40, GK 131*b*.

לכלכלך. Prep. *lamedh* plus inf. cstr. pilpel of כול (here 'nourish') plus 2 m. s. suffix. The tone is retracted in pause with *silluq* on to the previous vocal *shewa*, which now becomes *seghol*, DG 41 (§10, 4c, i), WL 117, GK 29*n*. There is now no need to open the vocal *shewa* under the second *kaph*, cf. the form which appears in verse 4.

Verse 10. **ויקם.** Pronounce *wăy-yā̆-qŏm*. Strong-*waw* plus 3 m. s. impf. (jussive) qal of קום (rise up). The ordinary impf. is יָקוּם, the jussive יָקֹם, and when this latter form is used with the strong-*waw* and the tone retracted on to the open pre-tone, the final long-*o* becomes short, DG 131 (§40, 2, b), WL 158.

ויבא. Strong-*waw* plus 3 m. s. impf. qal of בוא (come).

15

פתח. Cstr. sing. of פֶּתַח (opening, doorway), same form as absolute.

הָעִיר. Article plus עִיר (city), *qamets* before ordinary *ayin* (i.e. *ayin-without-qamets*).

מְקֹשֵׁשׁ. Fem. sing. of poel ptc. מְקוֹשֵׁשׁ from קשׁשׁ, a denominative (i.e. formed from the noun) verb from קַשׁ (stubble). The strict meaning is 'gathering stubble', but here more generally of gathering odd sticks. The poel is the usual intensive form of a double-*ayin* verb. It is not distinguishable in form from the intensive form of an *ayin-waw* verb, which is called polal, because the last radical is doubled, DG 138 and 132, WL 166 and 160.

עֵצִים. Pl. of עֵץ (tree). The plural tends to mean 'logs' (cf. Latin *ligna*) or pieces of wood suitable for firewood, GK 124*l*, DS 19 (Rem 1).

וַיִּקְרָא. Strong-*waw* plus 3 m. s. impf. qal of קרא I (call).

אֵלֶיהָ. Prep. אֶל (to) plus 3 f. s. suffix. This prep., like עַל (upon), appears to take plural suffixes, DG 70, WL 64f.

וַיֹּאמֶר. Strong-*waw* plus 3 m. s. impf. qal of אמר (say). The tone is not retracted here (cf. note in verse 1) because the clause ends, so that the accent is disjunctive (*zaqeph-qaton*). The last vowel thus remains *pathach*, as in the paradigm, DG 215, WL 257.

קְחִי. 2 f. s. imperat. qal of לקח (take). The verb

16

acts as if *pe-nun*, DG 213, WL 255. The following word
נא is a particle of entreaty.

לִי. Prep. *lamedh* plus 1 s. suffix, DG 51, WL 49.

מְעַט. Substantive meaning 'fewness, a little', used
regularly, as here, in construct with noun following.

בכלי. Prep. *beth* plus article plus כְּלִי (vessel). For
suffixes, DG 153, WL 186. The suffixes of the singular
noun are as if the noun is 3rd declension (vocal *shewa*
before tone), but those of the plural noun are based on
a 1st declension form כֵּלִים (long vowel in pretone).

ואשתה. Weak-*waw* (denoting purpose, cf. ἵνα) plus
1 s. impf. qal of שתה (drink), DG 86, WL 91, DS 90,
DT 64–67: 'in order that I may drink'.

Verse 11. ותלך. Strong-*waw* plus 3 f. s. impf. qal of הלך
(go, walk) with tone retracted and last vowel shortened
(note in verse 5).

לקחת. Prep. *lamedh* (with *qamets*, DG 51, WL 45)
plus קַחַת, inf. cstr. qal of לקח (take). The *lamedh* is not
the *lamedh* of the root, which drops out after the pattern
of *pe-nun* verbs with impf. in -*a*, DG 114 (top), WL 130.

לקחי. 2 f. s. imperat. qal of לקח (take). The usual
form omits the *lamedh* (cf. in verse 10). Some would
read here לָהּ קְחִי '(and he said) to her, Take . . .'.

פת. Cstr. sing. of פַּת (morsel), same form as absolute.

בידך. Prep. *beth* plus 2 f. s. suffix to sing. יָד (hand).
Verse 12. ותאמר. Strong-*waw* plus 3 f. s. impf. qal of אמר

(say), with tone retracted and *seghol* for *pathach* in last syllable, DG 119, WL 172.

אלהיך. 2 m. s. suffix to plural form אֱלֹהִים (god), plural of majesty, GK 124g, DS 18.

אם introducing the substance of the oath; see note in verse 1.

יֶשׁ־. The noun יֵשׁ means 'being', and is used often as if it were a verb meaning 'is, are'. Here the vowel is shortened because of the following *maqqeph*; see note in verse 3.

מעוג. Noun meaning 'cake', i.e. circular cake. Targum and Syriac read מְאוּמָה (anything), which may well be right.

כי אם after an implied negative; see note in verse 1.

מלא. Noun meaning 'fulness', here cstr. sing. with same form as absolute.

כף. Noun meaning 'hollow' of hand or foot. Here cstr. sing., having same form as absolute, 'a handful of meal'.

בכד. Prep. *beth* plus article plus כַּד (jar), originally a mortar in which things are pounded.

ומעט. *Waw*-copula (-*u* before labial, b-u-m-p) plus noun meaning 'a little'.

בצפחת. Prep. *beth* plus צַפַּחַת (jar), the shape being wide and flat. Note *qamets* for *pathach* in pause with *athnach*, DG 40, WL 117.

וְהִנֵּנִי. *Waw*-copula plus הִנֵּה (behold) plus 1 s. suffix, DG 142, WL 110f.

שְׁנַיִם. Numeral masc. 'two'. The rules for cardinal numerals are: 1 agrees in gender, is an adjective, and follows the noun; 2 agrees in gender, is in the construct, and precedes the noun; 3–10, with the article, differ in gender, are in the construct, and precede the noun; 3–10 without the article, differ in gender, are in the absolute, and precede the noun. The 'tens' are always masculine and precede the noun. All, except of course 1, take the plural, though 11–18 take the singular with words of time, measure, weight, etc., and there is a general tendency to use the singular. Say 'twenty and three' for the best classical style. The 'tens' take the singular only in Ezekiel and P. There are many variations from these rules, but these represent the average usage, DG 163f, WL 194f, DS 50–57, GK 134.

וּבָאתִי. Strong-*waw* (-*u* before labial) plus 1 s. pf. qal of בּוֹא (come).

וַעֲשִׂיתִהוּ. Strong-*waw* (with *pathach* to complete the pattern before *chateph-pathach*, DG 51, WL 43) plus 1 s. pf. qal of עשׂה (do, make, 'prepare' of food) plus 3 m. s. suffix.

וְלִבְנִי. *Waw*-copula plus prep. *lamedh* plus 1 s. suffix to the sing. בֵּן (son). This noun acts as 3rd declension in the sing., and as 1st declension in plural with form בָּנִים, DG 153, WL 186. LXX and Lucian both have the plural.

וַאֲכָלֻנְהוּ. Strong-*waw* plus 1 pl. pf. qal of אכל (eat) plus 3rd sing. suffix. The final -*u* of the verbal form is here written defectively, DG 20, WL 12.

19

ומתנו. Strong-*waw* (*qamets* before the tone and at the end of a sentence, DG 53, WL 45, especially GK 104*g*; normally the vowel is -*u*) plus 1 pl. pf. qal מַתְנוּ of מוּת (die), with *qamets* for *pathach* in pause with *silluq* at the end of the verse.

Verse 13. אַל־תִּירְאִי. אַל with the jussive means 'don't'; לֹא with the imperfect means 'thou shalt not', a strong prohibition, DG 83, WL 77f, DS 86, GK 109*c–e* and 107*c*.

תִּירְאִי. 2 f. s. impf. qal of יָרֵא (be afraid).

בֹּאִי. 2 f. s. imperat. qal of בּוֹא (come), followed by similar form of עשׂה (do, make, prepare).

עֻגָה. Fem. noun meaning 'cake' (shape of disc). Some texts have a *dagesh* in the *gimel*, but this is wrong. The vowel is long because the root from which the noun developed is *ayin-waw*, DG 136, WL 190 (top). In this instance, the scribes did not happen to insert the *waw* for the long -*u* at the time when they first used *he*, *waw* and *yodh* for the unchangeably long vowels, DG 11f, WL 11, GK 7*b*.

קְטַנָּה. Fem. sing. of adj. קָטָן (little). The final radical is sharpened (doubled) in order to keep the previous vowel short, DG 141, WL 55, especially GK 93*ee*.

בָּרִאשֹׁנָה. Prep. *beth* plus article (*qamets* always before *resh*) plus fem. sing. of adj. רִאשׁוֹן (former, first), the whole form being used regularly as an adverbial phrase 'at first, first of all'.

20

והוצאת. Strong-*waw* plus 2 f. s. pf. hiphil of יצא (go out), 'and bring out (to me)', the perfect being consecutive from an original imperative, GK 112*r*, DT 124f, DS 81. The clause finishes with the following word and the accent *zaqeph-qaton* (like a *shewa* above the word); i.e. first make a cake for me, and later make a cake for yourself and your son. The problem of the *lamedh-aleph* verbs is wholly concerned with the vowel before the *aleph*, which quiesces at the end of a closed syllable. What does the vowel become? Think of the top line of the perfects and of the qal on the left as two containing walls, DG 220f, WL 262f. Pick out the 3 m. s. perfects of piel and hithpael (which have *tsere*), the imperfects of pual and hophal (which have *qamets*), all the 3 f. plurals and all the 2 f. plurals of the imperfects (which have *seghol*). For the rest: along the top of the paradigm and down the left, the vowel is *qamets*; always inside the containing 'walls' the vowel is *tsere*. The hiphil -*i* holds, as usual, with vowel endings; imperatives, participles and all infinitives follow the normal rules.

ולך. *Waw*-copula plus prep. *lamedh* plus 2 f. s. suffix, DG 51, WL 49. If the translation was 'to me and to thee', the Hebrew would be לִי וָלָךְ, DG 53 (§15, 1, d), WL 45. The Hebrew connects לך with what follows.

ולבנך. *Waw*-copula plus prep. *lamedh* plus 2 f. s. suffix to sing. בֵּן. LXX and Lucian have the plural here, as before.

תעשׂי. 2 f. s. impf. qal of עשׂה (do, prepare).

באחרנה. This word is the counterpart of the previous בראשׁנה: first make me a cake, and later make yourselves one. The adjective is אַחֲרוֹן (late).

Verse 14. כי. Conjunction 'for', very like the Greek ὅτι.

כה. Adverb 'thus', used regularly in this phrase.

תכלה. 3 f. s. impf. qal of כלה (be complete, at an end). The final vowel of a *lamedh-he* verb should be *seghol*, but here the *lamedh-aleph* model is followed, GK 75*rr*.

תחסר. 3 f. s. impf. qal of חָסַר (be lacking), but with *qamets* for *pathach* in pause with *athnach*, DG 40, WL 117.

עד. Prep. 'to' of time (as here) and space.

יום. Cstr. sing. of יוֹם (day), same form as absolute. The rest of the verse acts as absolute to this construct, lit. 'to the day of the-giving-of-the-LORD-. . .'. This construction shows why this infinitive is called inf. cstr., i.e. the form has to be translated 'the giving of . . .'.

תתן. The Kethib (what is written, DG 41, WL 119) is תֵּתֵן, unless this is an early error for תֵּנָת. The same form is found in 1 Kings 6¹⁹, GK 66*i*. The Qere (what is read, DG 41, WL 119) is תֵּת, normal inf. cstr. qal of נתן (give), DG 213, WL 255.

האדמה. Article (*qamets* before *aleph*) plus אֲדָמָה (ground). The word can be used of the ground generally, but strictly it means the tilled ground as against the untilled wilderness (מִדְבָּר).

Verse 15. וַתַּעֲשֶׂה. Strong-*waw* plus 3 f. s. impf. qal of
עשׂה (do, make, prepare). The impf. of a *lamedh-he* verb
is usually apocopated with strong-*waw* (DG 147, WL
144), but this is one of four cases of this form where the
full impf. is retained.

וַתֹּאכַל. Strong-*waw* plus 3 f. s. impf. qal of אכל (eat).
The final *pathach* is retained even when the tone is
retracted with strong-*waw*, GK 68*d*. The *seghol* is found
only when the verb is אמר, WL 172 (note 1), DG 119.

הוּא וְהִיא. The Kethib is הוּא וָהִיא (he and she), but
the Qere is הִיא וָהוּא (she and he). The latter is better
syntactically, the verb thus agreeing in gender with the
nearest subject, GK 146*f*, DS 158. The *waw*-copula has
qamets because it is in the pretone and in a pair, DG 53,
WL 45.

וּבֵיתָהּ. *Waw*-copula (-*u* before labial) plus 3 f. s.
suffix to sing. בַּיִת (house). Possibly we should read
וּבְנָהּ (and her son), cf. verses 12, 13, 17, where LXX has
the plural as here, i.e. in all four cases.

יָמִים. Plural of יוֹם (day), DG 153, WL 186. This
word is not in the Hexapla. If the text is sound, then
the word is used by itself of an indefinite period of time,
a use supported elsewhere only in Neh. 1[4]. Possibly we
ought to read יֹם יֹם, i.e. יוֹם יוֹם (day by day), Gen. 39[10]
etc. The plural by itself usually means 'a year'.

Verse 16. כלתה. 3 f. s. pf. qal (כָּלְתָה) of כלה (be complete, at an end), but with tone retracted in pause with
zaqeph-qaton, and with *qamets* for vocal *shewa*, DG 40*f*,
WL 117, GK 29*m*.

חָסֵר. Ordinary 3 m. s. pf. qal of a stative verb (be lacking). The paradigms can be misleading here. The stative is not an alternative form to the active qal. A stative verb is a verb which describes a state (to be lacking, to be small, to be heavy, etc.) and is usually intransitive. Such verbs usually have a pf. qal in -*e* (occasionally in -*o*) and an impf. qal in -*a*. Normal transitive verbs are like קטל, with a pf. qal in -*a* and not in -*e*, and an impf. qal in -*o* and not in -*a*.

Verse 17. חלה. 3 m. s. pf. qal, normal *lamedh-he* form, 'was ill'.

בעלת. Cstr. sing. of בַּעֲלָה (mistress), fem. 2nd declension (segholate) noun.

הבית. Article plus בַּיַת (house), with *qamets* for *pathach* in pause with *athnach*, DG 40, WL 117.

חליו. 3 m. s. suffix to sing. חֲלִי (sickness), a *lamedh-he* noun, second declension, DG 148, WL 189.

עד אשר is a conjunction meaning 'to'. The relative אשר has been added to the prep. עד in order to make the conjunction, so that it is followed by a finite verb. If the relative is not used, the following verb would normally be an inf. cstr.

נותרה. 3 f. s. pf. niphal of יתר (remain over). For *dagesh* in following *beth*, see note on לך in verse 3.

נשמה is ordinary quiet breathing as against רוּחַ (spirit, wind), which, when used of 'breath', means violent noisy breathing as in anger.

24

Verse 18. מה is the interrogative 'what? how?', DG 48,
WL 39. The precise rules for pointing are most com-
plicated (GK 37*a–f*), but the general rules are: Before
ordinary consonants and before *aleph* and *resh*, as for the
article; before all other gutturals, with *pathach*; but for
gutturals-with-*qamets*, with *seghol* by dissimilation.

מה לי ולך. The whole phrase is lit. 'what to me and
to thee?' Cf. John 2⁴ τί ἐμοὶ καὶ τοί, a true Semitism.
לך is prep. *lamedh* plus 2 f. s. suffix, and the preceding
copula has the vowel *qamets* because it is in the pretone
in a pair, DG 53, WL 45.

איש האלהים. 'O man of God'. The article is attached
to the absolute and not to the construct, following the
strict and rigorous rule (DG 60, WL 59), and here
expresses the vocative, DS 27, GK 126*f*.

באת. 2 m. s. pf. qal of בוא (come).

להזכיר. Prep. *lamedh* plus inf. cstr. hiphil of זכר
(remember).

עוני. 1 s. suffix to sing. עָוֹן (iniquity).

ולהמית. *Waw*-copula (-*u* before vocal *shewa*) plus
prep. *lamedh* plus inf. cstr. hiphil of מות (die).

בני. 1. sing. suffix to singular בֵּן (son), DG 153, WL
186. The suffixes to the sing. follow 3rd declension
rules.

Verse 19. תני. 2 f. s. imperat. qal of נתן (give), DG 213,
WL 255.

וַיִּקָּחֵהוּ. Strong-*waw* plus 3 m. s. impf. qal of לָקַח (take) plus 3 m. s. suffix. The vowel under the *qoph* is *qamets* because the verbal form ends in -*a* and thus follows first declension rules. Verbal forms ending in -*e* and -*o* follow third declension rules.

מֵחֵיקָהּ. Prep. *min* (*tsere* before guttural, DG 52, WL 32) plus sing. חֵיק (bosom) plus 3 f. s. suffix. Note the *mappiq* (DG 33, WL 9) in the *he* of the 3 f. s. suffix.

וַיַּעֲלֵהוּ. Strong-*waw* plus 3 m. s. impf. hiphil of עלה (go up) plus 3 m. s. suffix. The form might be the impf. qal (note the *pathach*s), but since the verb is obviously transitive, it must be the hiphil. The qal of this verb is necessarily intransitive.

הָעֲלִיָּה. Article (*qamets* before ordinary *ayin*) plus עֲלִיָּה (upper room), a small room built on the roof with access from the street and not from inside the house.

יֹשֵׁב. Act. ptc. qal of יָשַׁב (dwell).

וַיִּשְׁכִּבֵהוּ. Strong-*waw* plus 3 m. s. impf. hiphil of שכב (lie down) plus 3 m. s. suffix. The form with strong-*waw* without suffix is וַיַּשְׁכֵּב with a *tsere*, but the hiphil -*i* returns when the suffix is added, WL 152, GK 60*g*.

מִטָּתוֹ. 3 m. s. suffix to the singular מִטָּה (bed, couch). *Verse* 20. **וַיֹּאמֶר**. Strong-*waw* plus 3 m. s. impf. qal of אמר (say), but without tone retracted, because the word is at the end of a clause. The last vowel thus remains *pathach*.

אֱלֹהָי. 1 s. suffix (*qamets* for *pathach* in pause with *zaqeph qaton*) to the plural form אלהים (God).

26

הגם. Interrogative-*he* plus particle גַּ (also, even). The pointing of this interrogative is: before ordinary consonants, the vowel is *chateph-pathach*; before *shewa* or the gutturals (including *aleph* and *resh*), the vowel is *pathach*; but if the guttural vowel is *qamets*, the vowel is *seghol* by dissimilation.

מתגורר. Masc. sing. ptc. hithpolel of גּוּר I (sojourn).

עמה. Prep. עָם (with) plus 3 f. s. suffix, i.e. 'with whom' (combined with the preceding relative אֲשֶׁר). For suffixes to this prep., DG 142, WL 49. The root is double-*ayin*; hence *dagesh* in *mem*.

הרעות. 2 m. s. pf. hiphil of רעע (be evil), intransitive in qal, transitive in hiphil. The normal form is הֲסִבּוֹתָ, but since the *ayin* cannot be doubled, the *chireq* is lengthened to *tsere*.

Verse 21. ויתמדד. Strong-*waw* plus 3 m. s. impf. hithpoel of מדד (measure), 'he measured himself', i.e. stretched himself out upon the boy. LXX and Lucian here have καὶ ἐνεφύσησεν (and he breathed), guessing, interpreting, or possibly reading וַיִּפַּח, strong-*waw* plus 3 m. s. impf. qal of נפח (breathe, blow).

שלש. Masc. cardinal 'three'. It precedes a fem. noun without the article, and is therefore in the absolute and masculine, see note on verse 12. פעמים is plural of פַּעַם (footbeat, occurrence, time).

תָּשָׁב. Pronounce *tā́-shŏbh*; 3 f. s. jussive qal (with tone retracted) of שׁוּב (return), 'let return'. The tone is retracted to prevent the two accented syllables coming

27

together, DG 41 (§10, 4. iii), WL 117f. The regular
3 f. s. impf. qal is תָּשׁוּב; the jussive is normally תָּשֹׁב.

נפשׁ, commonly translated 'soul', but is properly the
breath-soul (Lat. *anima*) which gives life to man. There
is no *nephesh* beyond the grave; it ceases with death.
The word 'soul', in both O.T. and N.T., has nothing
to do with any immortal part in man's nature. It is
essentially mortal.

קרבו. 3 m. s. suffix to the singular קֶרֶב (midst). The
preceding prep. עַל (upon, against) should properly be
אֶל (to). The two words are often confused.

Verse 22. וישׁמע. Strong-*waw* plus 3 m. s. impf. qal of
שׁמע (hear), not often found with prep. *beth*; often used
as here in sense of 'hear and answer'.

ותשׁב. Strong-*waw* plus 3 f. s. jussive (tone retracted)
qal of שׁוּב (return). For retraction of tone with impf.
and strong-*waw*, DG 85 (bottom), WL 90. See note on
previous verse. Pronounce *wăt-tā-shŏbh*.

ויחי. Strong-*waw* plus 3 m. s. impf. (apoc.) qal of
חיה (live). The normal apoc. form is יְחִי, so that the
normal strong-*waw* form is וַיְחִי, with *dagesh* failing in
yodh-with-*shewa*, DG 32f and 147f, WL 20 and 145. The
pausal form is יֶחִי, WL 145 (note 2), GK 29*n*, 75*s*, so
that *dagesh* does not now fail, and we get the form וַיֶּחִי.
Verse 23. ויקח. Strong-*waw* plus 3 m. s. impf. qal of לקח
(take), DG 213, WL 255. The *lamedh* assimilates as in
pe-nun verb, DG 213, WL 255.

28

וירדהו. Strong-*waw* plus 3. m. s. impf. hiphil of ירד (go down) plus 3 m. s. suffix. Without suffix the form is יֹרִד, but the hiphil -*i* returns with the suffix, WL 152, GK 60*g*.

הביתה. Article plus בַּיִת (house) plus toneless *he-locale* of 'direction towards', DG 61f, WL 55, 211.

ויתנהו. Strong-*waw* plus 3 m. s. impf. qal of נתן (give), plus 3 m. s. suffix, DG 213, WL 255.

לאמו. Prep. *lamedh* plus 3 m. s. suffix to sing. אֵם (mother). The root is double-*ayin*, DG 140 (like חֵץ), WL 190 (like לֵב).

ראי. 2 f. s. imperat. qal of ראה (see), normal *lamedh-he* form.

חי. Adjective masc. sing., but it might possibly be 3 m. s. pf. qal of חיה (live). The root was originally חיי, so that pf. qal can be either the double-*ayin* form חַי (24 times) or the *lamedh-he* form חָיָה (5 times).

Verse 24. עתה זה 'now indeed'. The demonstrative זֶה is used idiomatically to add emphasis, DS 5, GK 136*c*.

אתה. 2 m. s. personal pronoun; *qamets* for *pathach* in pause with *athnach*, DG 40, WL 117.

בפיך. Prep. *beth* (in) plus 2 m. s. suffix to sing. פֶּה (mouth), DG 153, WL 186.

CHAPTER XVIII

Verse 1. וַיְהִי. Strong-*waw* plus 3 m. s. impf. (apoc.) qal of היה (be): 'and there were many days'. The usual phrase is וַיְהִי מִיָּמִים רַבִּים (Josh. 23[1], etc.), 'and it came to pass after (מִן, lit. "from") many days', so Targum and a few MSS.

רבים. Masc. pl. of רַב, adjective 'many'. The root is double-*ayin*, hence *dagesh-forte* in the *beth*.

ודבר. *Waw*-copulative (-*u* before *shewa*, DG 53, WL 44) plus cstr. sing. of דָּבָר (word).

בשנה. Prep. *beth* plus article plus שָׁנָה (year).

השלישית. Article plus fem. ordinal 'third'. Masc. is שְׁלִישִׁי. There are two fem. forms, שְׁלִישִׁית and שְׁלִישָׁה, DG 165, WL 197. This and the previous word are probably an interpolation.

לֵךְ. 2 m. s. imperat. qal of הלך (go), one of six like יֵשֵׁב; see note on 17[3].

הראה. 2 m. s. imperat. niphal of ראה (see). The normal form is הִקָּטֵל, but the *resh* cannot be doubled, so the previous *chireq* is lengthened to *tsere*; and the final vowel is *tsere*, because the verb is *lamedh-he*; lit. 'be seen', 'appear'.

ואתנה. Weak-*waw* plus 1 s. impf. (cohortative, DG 83, WL 85f) qal of נתן (give), DG 213, WL 255.

פְנֵי. Cstr. pl. of פָּנִים (face, faces), found only in plural.

Verse 2. וַיֵּלֶךְ. Strong-*waw* plus 3 m. s. impf. qal of הלך (go), one of six verbs like יֵשֵׁב; tone retracted with strong-*waw* and final vowel (now after the tone) shortened, DG 85, WL 90. See note on 17[5].

לְהֵרָאוֹת. Prep. *lamedh* plus inf. cstr. niphal of ראה (see). The *tsere* occurs because *resh* cannot be doubled, and *-oth* is the regular ending of the inf. cstr. of *lamedh-he* verbs.

וְהָרָעָב. Ordinary *waw* plus article plus masc. noun רָעָב (famine).

חָזָק. Adjective; root means 'get, have a firm hold'.

Verse 3. הַבַּיִת. Article plus בַּיִת (house) with *qamets* for *pathach* in pause with *athnach*, DG 40, WL 117.

יָרֵא. This is the act. ptc. qal of the stative verb יָרֵא (be afraid, fear), since it is followed by an accusative. Otherwise it might be an adjective. With the pf. qal הָיָה, it forms a composite tense, expressing continuance of a state, GK 116*r*, DS 136. The construction is quite common in late Hebrew.

Verse 4. בְּהַכְרִית. Prep. *beth* plus inf. cstr. hiphil of כרת (cut, cut off).

נְבִיאֵי. Cstr. plural of נָבִיא (prophet).

וַיִּקַּח. See note on 17[23].

31

מאה. Numeral (hundred), usually found in absolute, the cstr. being found only in P, DG 165, WL 196. This numeral is normally followed by the sing. (cf. verse 13), but here the plural is used, so that the LXX ἄνδρας may actually stand for an original אֲנָשִׁים, i.e. 'a hundred men, prophets'; cf. the construction 'a woman, a widow' in 17⁹.

ויחביאם. Strong-*waw* plus 3 m. s. impf. hiphil of חבא (hide) plus 3 m. pl. suffix.

חמשים. Numeral (fifty). If the meaning is 'by fifties in a cave', the numeral should be repeated, cf. verse 13. So LXX, Syriac and Targum (Lagarde's edition). For such 'distributives', WL 198, DS 56.

במערה. Prep. *beth* plus article plus fem. noun מְעָרָה (cave). The root is ערר I (double-*ayin*), so that the first *qamets* is firm, i.e. the cstr. sing. is מְעָרַת. The article is used because the writer is thinking of the particular cave which happened to be involved, GK 126*q*, DS 25. In English we use the indefinite article in such cases.

וכלכלם. Strong-*waw* plus 3 m. s. pf. pilpel of כּוּל (contain) plus 3 m. pl. suffix. The pilpel of this root usually means 'sustain, nourish', cf. 17⁴. The previous verb is impf. with strong-*waw* of one particular action; this verb is pf. with strong-*waw* of repeated action. Some would read וַיְכַלְכְּלֵם, which is easier (see verse 13), strong-*waw* plus 3 m. s. impf. pilpel, following naturally on the previous verb.

וָמָיִם. The *waw* has *qamets*, being before the tone and

32

in a pair, DG 53, WL 46. It is followed by *qamets* for *pathach* in pause with *silluq* at the end of the verse, DG 40, WL 117.

Verse 5. After לך, insert וְנַעֲבֹר (and let us traverse) with LXX, as is demanded by the following נמצא. The inserted word is weak-*waw* plus 1 pl. impf. qal of עבר (cross over).

בארץ. Prep. *beth* plus article plus אֶרֶץ (land), DG 46, WL 27.

כָּל־. The word כֹּל strictly is the cstr. sing. of the noun כֹּל (the whole), and is used for 'all'. Usually it is joined to the following word by *maqqeph* (DG 40, WL 28), in which case it is reckoned as part of the next word, and the vowel (normally long) becomes short (DG 48, WL 61), being now in a closed syllable without the tone.

מעיני. Cstr. pl. of מַעְיָן (spring). The plural normally is in -*oth* in spite of the noun being masc.

הנחלים. Article plus plural of masc. noun נַחַל (wady).

אולי. Adverb (perhaps).

נמצא. 1 pl. impf. qal of מצא (find).

חציר. General word for '*green* grass, herbage'.

ונחיה. Weak-*waw* (-*u* before *shewa*, DG 53, WL 45) plus 1 pl. impf. piel of חיה (live); equivalent to Greek

c   33

ἵνα, 'in order that we may keep alive', DG 86, WL 91, DS 90, DT 64–67.

סוס ופרד, 'war-horse and mule'. The *waw*-copula has *qamets*, being in the pretone and in a pair, DG 53, WL 45.

ולוא. *Waw*-copula plus ordinary negative לא, this being one of five times in this book when the *waw* of the *cholem* is written. The whole phrase is difficult; lit. 'and not cause to cut off from the cattle', i.e. and not have some of the cattle killed. The construction can barely stand, though it is not generally viewed with favour. Perhaps we should follow Lucian and read וְלֹא תִכָּרֵת מִמֶּנּוּ בְהֵמָה 'and (the) cattle not be cut off from us'.

מהבהמה. Prep. *min* (*tsere* before consonant which cannot be doubled, DG 52, WL 32) plus article plus fem. noun בְּהֵמָה (beast, often 'domestic beast' as against 'wild beasts'). Many editions follow Jacob-ben-Chayim and read מִן־הַבְּהֵמָה. The *min* is 'partitive', WL 208, DS 141.

Verse 6. ויחלקו. Strong-*waw* (*dagesh* failing in *yodh*-with-*shewa*, DG 32f, WL 20) plus 3 m. pl. impf. piel of חלק (divide), 'so they divided the land between them'. The *dagesh* often fails also in *lamedh*-with-*shewa* (DG 32, WL 20), but not here.

את־הארץ. LXX, Lucian and Syriac apparently read אֶת־הַדֶּרֶךְ (the road, way), but MT is better. Possibly they were 'correcting', cf. the following בדרך (twice).

לעבר־. Prep. *lamedh* plus inf. cstr. qal of עבר (traverse) with short-*o* because of *maqqeph*, DG 40, WL 28.

34

אחד. The double use of this masc, numeral (one) is equivalent to the English 'the one . . . the other'.

לבדו. Prep. *lamedh* plus noun בַּד (separation) plus 3 m. s. suffix. The form לְבַד is used regularly for 'by itself, himself', etc. The root is double-*ayin*, hence *dagesh-forte* with suffix. The first of the two occurrences is omitted in LXX and Lucian.

Verse 7. לקראתו. Prep. *lamedh* plus קְרָאת, inf. cstr. qal of קרא II (encounter) plus 3 m. s. suffix. The inf. cstr. qal of קרא I (call) is קְרֹא.

ויכרהו. Strong-*waw* plus 3 m. s. impf. hiphil of נכר I (recognise) plus 3 m. s. suffix. LXX and Lucian both have καὶ ἔσπευσεν, as if reading וימהר, strong-*waw* plus 3 m. s. impf. piel of מהר (hasten).

ויפל. Strong-*waw* plus 3 m. s. impf. qal of נפל (fall).

פניו. Plural פָּנִים (face) plus 3 m. s. suffix.

האתה. Interrogative *he* plus 2 m. sing. pronoun (thou). For pointing of interrog. *he*, see note on 17[19].

זה. Masc. demonstrative pronoun, here used as an enclitic to emphasise the interrogative, WL 36, DS 7, GK 136c.

אדני. Sing. noun אָדוֹן (lord) plus 1 sing. suffix.

Verse 8. אָנִי. Pausal form of אֲנִי, 1 sing. personal pronoun, DG 41, WL 41. The word is omitted by Lucian.

אמר. 2 m. s. imperat. qal of אמר (say).

לאדניך. Prep. *lamedh* plus plural of אָדוֹן (lord) plus
2 m. s. suffix. Before the inseparable prepositions and
also before *waw*-copulative, the *aleph* of אדון, in all forms
with suffix, becomes quiescent, and the prefix takes
pathach, WL 45. Add this to the exceptions given in
DG 51, §14 (c). The plural refers to Ahab the king,
and is called 'plural of majesty', DS 18, GK 124k.

Verse 9. מה. Interrogative pronoun (what? how?). For
pointing, see note in 17¹⁸.

חטאתי. 1 s. pf. qal of חטא (err, sin).

נתן. Act. ptc. qal of נתן (give).

עבדך. 2 m. s. suffix to sing. of עֶבֶד (servant, slave).

להמיתני. Prep. *lamedh* plus inf. cstr. hiphil of מות (die)
plus 1 s. suffix.

Verse 10. אם. Introduces the substance of the oath.
See note on 17¹.

יש־. See note on 17¹².

וממלכה. *Waw*-copula (-*u* before labial, b-u-m-p,
DG 53, WL 44) plus fem. noun מַמְלָכָה (kingdom).

אשר. Relative followed by adverb שָׁם (there) to
mean 'where'.

לבקשך. Prep. *lamedh* plus inf. cstr. piel of בקש (seek)
plus 2 m. s. suffix.

ואמרו. Strong-*waw* plus 3 m. pl. pf. qal of אמר (say).
This opens the protasis of a conditional sentence with
two perfects-with-strong-*waw*, 'and if they should say

36

No, then he would make (them) swear', WL 205, DS 176 and 180, DT 185, GK 159*s* and 112*ff*. The simplest type of conditional sentence has אִם-with-impf. in the protasis and pf.-with-strong-*waw* in the apodosis, but this can be varied (as here) by pf.-with-strong-*waw* in the protasis also: 'if I do this, then he will do that': I may or may not do the first, but if I do then the rest follows necessarily.

אִין. The word אַיִן is properly a noun meaning 'not-being', and is thus the opposite to יֵשׁ (see above). Here the meaning is 'No'. The *qamets* is due to the pause with *athnach*, DG 40, WL 117.

וְהִשְׁבִּעַ. Strong-*waw* plus 3 m. s. pf. hiphil of שׁבע (swear).

יִמְצָאֶכָּה. 3 m. s. impf. qal of מצא (find) plus *nun-energicum* (DG 110 § 31, 7; WL 150) plus 2 m. s. suffix with *qamets* written full (i.e. with *he*); 'that he could not find thee', DG 78 (bottom), WL 67, DT 42, DS 64f, GK 107*k*.

Verse 11. הנה אליהו. LXX omits.

Verse 12. וְהָיָה. Strong-*waw* plus 3 m. s. pf. qal, 'and it will happen (come to be)'.

אֵלֵךְ. 1 s. impf. qal of הלך (go), almost 'if I go . . . then the spirit of the Lord will carry thee . . .'

מֵאִתְּךָ. Prep. *min* (*tsere* before consonant which cannot be doubled, DG 52, WL 32) plus prep. אֵת (with) plus 2 m. s. suffix in pause (normally אִתְּךָ), DG 142, WL 49.

37

ורוח. *Waw*-copula plus cstr. sing. of fem. (except once) noun רוּחַ (wind, spirit). Construct singular has same form as absolute.

יִשָּׂאֲךָ. 3 m. s. impf. qal of נשׂא (lift up, carry) plus 2 m. s. suffix.

על. Either an error for prep. אֶל (to) or a pregnant construction for '*carry thee* up and set thee down *upon*'.

אדע. 1 s. impf. qal of ידע (know), one of six *pe-yodh* verbs like יֵשֵׁב.

ובאתי. Strong-*waw* plus 1 s. pf. qal of בּוֹא (come). A conditional sentence begins here, the apodosis beginning with והרגני. First type: 'If I come . . ., then he will kill me'; see note in 18¹⁰.

להגיד. Prep. *lamedh* plus inf. cstr. hiphil of נגד (tell, announce).

יִמְצָאֲךָ. 3 m. s. impf. qal of מצא (find) plus 2 m. s. suffix; continuing from the impf. implied in the pf.-with-strong-*waw* (ובאתי) which opens the protasis.

והרגני. Strong-*waw* plus 3 m. s. pf. qal of הרג (kill) plus 1 s. suffix, with *qamets* for *pathach* in pause with *athnach*.

מנעורי. Prep. *min* plus נְעוּרִים (youth) plus 1 s. suffix with *qamets* for *pathach* in pause with *silluq*. Forms like נעורים denote a time of life, e.g. זְקוּנִים (old age), בְּתוּלִים (maidenhood), GK 124*d*.

Verse 13. הלא. Interrogative *he* plus negative לא.

38

הֻגַּד. 3 m. s. pf. hophal of נגד (tell, announce). Note the short-*u* before the *dagesh*, characteristic of hophals of *pe-nun* verbs.

אֵת here introducing a whole clause as the definite object of the verb.

עָשִׂיתִי. 1 s. pf. qal of עשׂה (do), normal *lamedh-he* form.

בַּהֲרֹג. Prep. *beth* plus inf. cstr. qal of הרג (slay), DG 111, WL 100.

וָאַחְבִּא. Strong-*waw* (*qamets* before *aleph*) plus 1 s. impf. hiphil of חבא (hide), following on עָשִׂיתִי.

מִנְּבִיאֵי. Prep. *min*-partitive (WL 208) plus cstr. pl. of נָבִיא (prophet).

וָאֲכַלְכְּלֵם. Strong-*waw* plus 1 s. impf. pilpel of כּוּל (nourish: see note on 18⁹) plus 3 m. pl. suffix, 'and I nourished them'.

Verse 15. כִּי introducing the substance of the oath, equivalent to אִם לֹא, WL 201, GK 149*d*, DS 165, 'assuredly today I will appear to him'.

אֵרָאֶה. 1 s. impf. niphal of ראה (see).

אֵלָיו. Prep. אֶל (to) plus 3 m. s. suffix: see note on 17¹⁰.

Verse 16. וַיַּגֶּד־. Strong-*waw* plus 3 m. s. impf. hiphil of נגד (tell). Ordinary impf. hiphil is יַגִּיד, jussive יַגֵּד, which is used with strong-*waw* (DG 95, WL 90), but here with *seghol* for *tsere* because of the following *maqqeph*, DG 40, WL 28.

ויֵלֶךְ. LXX and Lucian prefix this with καὶ
ἐξέδραμεν, i.e. וַיָּרָץ, pronounced wăy-yā́-rŏts: strong-
waw plus 3 m. s. impf. qal of רוץ (run), 'and Ahab (ran
and) went . . .'

Verse 17. כראות. Prep. *kaph* plus inf. cstr. qal of ראה
(see).

עכר. Active ptc. qal of עכר (trouble).

Verse 18. כי אם is 'but' after a negative: see note on 17[1].

ובית. *Waw*-copulative (-*u* before labial) plus cstr.
sing. of בַּיִת (house), DG 153, WL 186.

אביך. Sing. noun אָב (father) plus 2 m. s. suffix, DG
153, WL 185. When the suffix-form has one 'dot' it is
the singular: 'one dot, one father', and similarly for אָח
(brother).

בעזבכם. Prep. *beth* plus inf. cstr. qal (the vowel is
short-*o*) of עזב (forsake) plus 2 m. pl. suffix: 'in that you
have forsaken'.

מצות. Cstr. pl. of fem. noun מִצְוָה (commandment).

ותלך. Strong-*waw* plus 2 m. s. impf. qal of הלך (go),
with tone retracted and final vowel shortened to *seghol*
from *tsere*, DG 85, WL 90.

אחרי. Construct dual (or plural) of noun אַחַר (the
after part), but used as prep. 'after'.

הבעלים. Article plus plural of masc. noun בַּעַל (lord,
husband), but used here of the gods of Canaan, referring
to the local identifications of the great god Baal.

40

Verse 19. שְׁלַח. 2 m. s. imperat. qal of שלח (send), followed by similar form of קבץ (gather).

אֵלַי. Prep. אֶל (to) plus 1 s. suffix, DG 70, WL 64f.

הַר. Cstr. sing. of הַר (mountain); a double-*ayin* root, so that the usual cstr. pl. is הָרֵי with firm *qamets* because *resh* cannot be doubled.

הכרמל. Article plus כַּרְמֶל (lit. 'the garden-land'), always with the article (DS 26, GK 126*e*), and always with short vowel in final syllable.

האשרה. Article plus אֲשֵׁרָה. It was formerly held that this word was used only of the sacred pole, once to be found close by an altar in association with a stone pillar, and that the use of the word in such a case of this (in conjunction with Baal) was a confusion of later times. The Ras Shamra tablets have made it clear that there was also a goddess named Asherah, and that even in pre-Hebrew times she was confused with Astarte.

אכלי. Masc. cstr. pl. of אֹכֵל, act. ptc. qal of אכל (eat).

שלחן. Cstr. sing. of masc. noun שֻׁלְחָן (table).

Verse 20. וישלח. Strong-*waw* plus 3 m. s. impf. qal of שלח (send).

ויקבץ. Strong-*waw* plus 3 m. s. impf. qal of קבץ (gather).

Verse 21. ויגש. Strong-*waw* plus 3 m. s. impf. qal of נגש (draw near).

41

מתי. Interrogative adverb (when?).

פֹסְחִים. Masc. pl. act. ptc. qal of פסח (limp).

שְׁתֵּי. Normal numeral 'two' before fem. noun: in construct and agreeing in gender. See note on 17¹².

הַסְּעִפִּים. Article plus pl. of fem. noun סְעִפָּה (division, divided opinion). See note in Burney, *Notes on the Hebrew Text of the Books of Kings*.

לְכוּ. 2 m. pl. imperat. qal of הלך (go); counts as one of six *pe-yodh* verbs with imperfects like יֵשֵׁב.

אַחֲרָיו. Prep. אַחֲרֵי (after) plus 3 m. s. suffix.

עָנוּ. 3 m. pl. pf. qal of ענה I (answer).

Verse 22. נוֹתַרְתִּי. I s. pf. niphal of יתר (remain over).

לַיהוה. Prep. *lamedh* plus the Sacred Name read as אֲדֹנָי (LORD). The *aleph* quiesces: cf. note on 18⁷.

לְבַדִּי. Prep. *lamedh* plus noun בַּד (separation) plus 1 s. suffix, the whole meaning 'by myself'. See note on 18⁶.

Verse 23. וִיתְּנוּ. Weak-*waw* plus 3 m. pl. impf. qal of נתן (give): 'and let them give', i.e. 'let there be given'.

לָנוּ. Prep. *lamedh* plus 1 pl. suffix, DG 51, WL 49.

שְׁנַיִם. Cardinal numeral for 'two'. This numeral always agrees in gender with its noun and is usually in construct, but it has a tendency (as here) to follow the rules for 3–10 and to be in the absolute when its noun is without the article. See note on 17¹².

פרים. Masc. pl. of פַּר (steer, bull), double-*ayin* root.

ויבחרו. Weak-*waw* plus 3 m. pl. impf. qal of בחר (choose): 'and let them choose'.

להם. Prep. *lamedh* plus 3 m. pl. suffix: ethic dative (WL 207, F (b), ii), 'for themselves'.

וינתחהו. Weak-*waw* plus 3 m. pl. impf. piel of נתח (cut in pieces, divide by the joints) plus 3 m. s. suffix.

וישימו. Weak-*waw* plus 3 m. pl. impf. qal of שִׂים (set).

העצים. Article plus plural of עֵץ (tree). The plural often means 'logs', WL 19 (Rem. 1).

ואש. *Waw*-copula plus noun אֵשׁ (fire), mostly fem. but occasionally masculine.

אעשה. 1 s. impf. qal of עשׂה (do, prepare).

ונתתי. Strong-*waw* plus 1 s. pf. qal of נתן (give, put).

אשים. 1 s. impf. qal of שִׂים (set).

Verse 24. וקראתם. Strong-*waw* (-*u* before *shewa*) plus 2 m. pl. pf. qal of קרא I (call aloud).

בשם. Prep. *beth* plus cstr. sing. of noun שֵׁם (name).

אקרא. 1 s. impf. qal of קרא I (call aloud).

יענה. 3 m. s. impf. qal of ענה I (answer).

באש. Prep. *beth* plus article (WL 26, GK 126*d*: English does not use the article here) plus אֵשׁ (fire).

ויען. Strong-*waw* plus 3 m. s. impf. qal (apoc.) of ענה
I (answer).

Verse 25. בחרו. 2 m. pl. imperat. qal of בחר (choose).

ועשו. *Waw*-copula (complete the pattern before the
chateph-vowel, DG 51, WL 43) plus 2 m. pl. imperat.
qal of עשה (do, prepare).

ראשנה. Fem. sing. of adj. ראשן (first), used as adverb,
a regular usage, whether of time, place or precedence.

הרבים. Article plus m. pl. of adjective רב (many),
double-*ayin* root: 'ye are the ones that are many.'

וקראו. *Waw*-copula plus 2 m. pl. imperat. qal of קרא
I (call aloud).

לא תשימו. לא with the impf. is a strong prohibition;
see note on 17¹³.

Verse 26. ויקחו. Strong-*waw* plus 3 m. pl. impf. qal
(*dagesh* fails in *qoph*-with-*shewa*, DG 33, WL 20) of לקח
(take), DG 213, WL 255.

נתן. 3 m. s. pf. qal of נתן (give), translated, as often
when immediately following אשר, as a pluperfect, DS
58 (39c), DT 22, GK 106*f*.

ויעשו. Strong-*waw* plus 3 m. pl. impf. qal of עשה
(do).

מהבקר. Prep. *min* (*tsere* before consonant which cannot be doubled, DG 52, WL 32) plus article plus בּקֶר
(morning, but see note on 17⁶).

44

הצהרים. Article plus צָהֳרַיִם (found only in this form), 'noon-day'. The form looks like the dual of a segholate צֹהַר, but is held actually to be a plural, GK 88*c*. The first vowel is short-*o*.

הבעל. The article expresses the vocative, WL 27, GK 126*f*.

ענגו. 2 m. s. imperat. qal (עֲנֵה) of ענה I (answer) plus 1 pl. suffix. LXX and Lucian repeat ἐπάκουσον ἡμῶν, probably under influence of verse 37, i.e. 'hear' in the sense of 'hear and answer'.

ואין. *Waw*-copula plus אֵין, cstr. s. of אַיִן, in frequent use as a particle of negation. See note on 18¹⁰.

עֹנֶה. Masc. s. act. ptc. qal of ענה I (answer), lit. 'nothing of one answering'.

ויפסחו. Strong-*waw* plus 3 m. pl. impf. piel (*dagesh* failing in *yodh*-with-*shewa*) of פסח (limp). LXX, Lucian and Vulgate understand 'exerted themselves'; Targum 'leapt madly'; evidently descriptive of a ritual dance peculiar to the worship of this Baal. See note in Burney.

המזבח. Article plus masc. noun מִזְבֵּחַ (altar).

עשה. 3 m. s. pf. qal of עשה (make), but this should certainly be עָשׂוּ (3 m. pl.) as in the Versions. So also the Sebhir, a suggestion of the Masoretes which falls short of the authority of a Qere. Translate as a pluperfect, DT 22, DS 58, GK 106*f*.

45

Verse 27. וַיְהָתֵל. Strong-*waw* plus 3 m. s. impf. piel (*dagesh* fails in *yodh*-with-*shewa*) of הָתַל (deceive, mock). This form is found only here, and may well be a secondary form (unless it is an error) of הֵתֵל, hiphil of the double-*ayin* verb תלל II, BDB 251 and 1068. GK 67*y* considers the form to be an Aramaizing form in which the *he* of the hiphil perfect is not elided in the imperfect.

שִׂיחַ. Noun (meditation), as Syriac. The other ancient Versions have 'conversation', cf. AV. The כִּי (and two following) is asserverative, 'surely', GK 159*ee*.

שִׂיג. If correct, for סִיג (moving back, temporary withdrawal), though this is the only use of the word (dross) in this sense. Generally explained as a euphemism, but the whole phrase וְכִי שִׂיג is not in LXX and Lucian, and is probably an accidental repetition of previous phrase.

וְכִי דֶרֶךְ לוֹ. Lit. 'and surely he has a journey'. The phrase is well paraphrased in LXX and Lucian, καὶ ἅμα μή ποτε χρηματίζει αὐτός, 'and perchance he has business to transact'.

יָשֵׁן. 3 m. s. pf. qal of stative verb יָשֵׁן (sleep, go to sleep), 'perhaps he has gone to sleep', though the form might be act. ptc. qal.

וְיִקָץ. Weak-*waw* plus 3 m. s. impf. qal of יקץ (awake): 'one must (should, DS 64, DT 43) awaken (him)'. The usual writing of this form is וַיִּיקַץ. The final vowel is lengthened to *qamets* in pause with *silluq*, DG 40, WL 117.

46

Verse 28. וַיִּתְגֹּדְדוּ. Strong-*waw* plus 3 m. pl. impf. hith-poel of גדד (cut).

כְּמִשְׁפָּטָם. Prep. *kaph* plus מִשְׁפָּט (strictly 'judgement according to precedent', and so 'custom') plus 3 m. pl. suffix.

בַּחֲרָבוֹת. Prep. *beth* plus article (the vowel would be *pathach* in any case, but see the following word) plus fem. pl. of fem. noun חֶרֶב (sword). The writer is thinking of the particular instruments they used, hence the use of the definite article, DS 26, GK 126*d*.

וּבָרְמָחִים. *Waw*-copula (-*u* before labial, b-u-m-p, DG 53, WL 44) plus prep. *beth* plus article plus pl. of masc. noun רֹמַח (short spear, lance)

עַד־שְׁפָך־. Prep. עַד (to), followed by inf. cstr. qal of שְׁפָךְ (pour out), with short-*o* because of the following *maqqeph*, DG 40, WL 28.

עֲלֵיהֶם. Prep. עַל (upon) plus 3 m. pl. suffix.

Verse 29. כַּעֲבֹר. Prep. *kaph* plus inf. cstr. qal of עבר (pass over).

וַיִּתְנַבְּאוּ. Strong-*waw* plus 3 m. pl. impf. hithpael of denominative verb נבא (act as a נָבִיא, prophet); the reference being to the raving ecstasy characteristic of Canaanite religion.

לַעֲלוֹת. Prep. *lamedh* plus inf. cstr. qal of עלה (go up); 'up to (עַד לְ) the offering up (lit. 'going up') of . . .'

47

המנחה. Article plus מִנְחָה (offering). In P, the minchah is the meal-offering which accompanied the meat-offering (the regular daily offering, dawn and evening). The meaning here is 'up to the time of the evening offering', which in later times was 3 p.m.

קשב. Noun (attentiveness), normally קֶשֶׁב, but with the primary vowel (*pathach*) lengthened to *qamets* in pause with *silluq*, DG 40, WL 117.

Verse 30. גשו. 2 m. pl. imperat. qal of נגש (draw near). The following verb is the same root, but strong-*waw* plus 3 m. pl. impf. qal.

וירפא. Strong-*waw* plus 3 m. s. impf. piel of רפא (heal, repair).

מזבח. Cstr. sing. (note *pathach*) of masc. noun מִזְבֵּחַ (altar).

ההרוס. Article plus pass. ptc. qal of הרס (thrown down).

Verse 31. שתים עשרה. Cardinal numeral (twelve) before fem. noun, DG 164, WL 196.

אבנים. Plural of fem. noun אֶבֶן (stone).

כמספר. Prep. *kaph* plus cstr. sing. of masc. noun מִסְפָּר (number).

שבטי. Cstr. pl. of masc. noun שֵׁבֶט (tribe).

אשר . . . אליו. The relative followed by אֵלָיו (to whom), DG 47, WL 38.

48

יִהְיֶה. 3 m. s. impf. qal of היה (be); first syllable is always open, DG 148, WL 145.

שְׁמֶךָ. This form is pausal for שִׁמְךָ, masc. 3rd declension noun שֵׁם (name) plus 2 m. s. suffix. The effect of the pause with *silluq* is to bring the tone forward on to the vocal *shewa*, which becomes *seghol*, DG 41, WL 117, GK 29n. The previous *shewa* need not now be raised to a *chireq* in a half-open syllable.

Verse 32. וַיִּבְנֶה. Strong-*waw* plus 3 m. s. impf. qal of בנה (build). This form is usually apocopated to become וַיִּבֶן, DG 146f, WL 144.

אֶת. Best regarded as a double accusative, DS 109, GK 117ii.

וַיַּעַשׂ. Strong-*waw* plus 3 m. s. impf. qal (apoc.) of עשׂה (make).

תְּעָלָה. Fem. noun (water-course, conduit), apparently here 'trench'.

כְּבֵית. Prep. *kaph* plus cstr. sing. of בַּיִת (house), here 'capacity'.

סָאתִים. Dual of סְאָה, a measure used for grain, flour, etc., about 10½ quarts. Followed by זֶרַע (seed), in apposition, DS 40, GK 131d.

סָבִיב. Noun used as adverb and (as here) as prep. 'round about'. In latter case usually followed by prep. *lamedh*.

Verse 33. וַיַּעֲרֹךְ. Strong-*waw* plus 3 m. s. impf. qal of עָרַךְ (set in order).

וַיְנַתַּח. Strong-*waw* plus 3 m. s. impf. piel (*dagesh* fails in *yodh-shewa*, DG 32, WL 20, as regularly in piel forms) of נתח (cut up at the joints).

וַיָּשֶׂם. Strong-*waw* plus 3 m. s. impf. qal of שִׂים (set, place). The normal 3 m. s. impf. qal is יָשִׂים; jussive is יָשֵׂם; when this is used with strong-*waw* (DG 95 and 85, WL 90), the tone is retracted, and *tsere* becomes *seghol*. The impf. qal of an *ayin-yodh* verb is indistinguishable in form from the impf. hiphil; the difference being detected usually by the fact that the qal is intransitive, and the hiphil transitive.

Verse 34. מִלְאוּ. 2 m. pl. imperat. qal of מָלֵא (fill).

אַרְבָּעָה. Cardinal numeral (four), before masc. noun without article, and therefore fem. and in absolute. See note on 17¹².

כַדִּים. Plural of masc. noun כַּד (jar), double-*ayin* root; hence the *dagesh-forte* in the *daleth*.

מַיִם. The second of the two accusatives governed by the verb (fill), GK 117*cc*. DS 108.

וַיִּצְקוּ. Weak-*waw* plus 3 m. pl. impf. qal of יצק (pour out, flow). This *pe-yodh* verb assimilates the *yodh* (יִצֹּק) as if it were a *pe-nun* verb like נפל, but here it has retained the *yodh* in the impf. qal יִיצֹק, though still with -*o* instead of the usual -*a*. The *metheg* insists on a long -*i*.

הַעֹלָה. Article plus fem. noun עֹלָה (whole burnt-offering), the term at every period for an offering wholly burnt on the altar.

שְׁנוּ. 2 m. pl. imperat. qal of שָׁנָה III (repeat, do a second time), followed by strong-*waw* plus 3 m. pl. impf. qal of same verb.

שִׁלֵּשׁוּ. 2 m. pl. imperat. piel (normally שַׁלְּשׁוּ) of denominative verb שִׁלֵּשׁ (do a third time), but here in pause with tone retracted, making the vocal *shewa* into the original *tsere*, DG 40 (bottom), WL 117. Followed by strong-*waw* (*dagesh* fails in *yodh*-with-*shewa*) plus 3 m. pl. impf. piel of same verb, normally וַיְשַׁלֵּשׁוּ, but once more in pause.

Verse 35. וַיֵּלְכוּ. Strong-*waw* plus 3 m. pl. impf. qal of הלך (go), which acts as a *pe-yodh* verb, being one of six like יֵשֵׁב.

מִלֵּא. 3 m. s. pf. piel of מָלֵא (fill, be full), presumably 'Elijah' being regarded as subject. LXX has plural, conforming to previous verb.

מִיִם. In pause for מַיִם (water), second object of verb 'fill'.

Verse 36. בַּעֲלוֹת. Prep. *beth* plus inf. cstr. qal of עלה (go up).

וַיִּגַּשׁ. Strong-*waw* plus 3 m. s. impf. qal of נגש (draw near).

הַיּוֹם. Article plus noun יוֹם (day): i.e. 'today'.

51

ויודע. 3 m. s. impf. niphal (*pathach* for *tsere* because of guttural) of ידע (know): 'let it be known'.

עבדך. 2 m. s. suffix to sing. of noun עֶבֶד (servant, slave), pausal form for the normal עַבְדְּךָ, DG 41, WL 117.

ובדבריך. *Waw*-copula (-*u* before labial, b-u-m-p, DG 51, WL 44) plus prep. *beth* (half-open syllable before *shewa*, DG 50, WL 43) plus masc. noun דָּבָר (word) plus 2 m. s. suffix. The Kethib is the plural, and the Qere is the singular.

Verse 37. ענני. 2 m. s. imperat. qal (עֲנֵה) of ענה I (answer) plus 1 s. suffix.

וידעו. Weak-*waw* (ĭνα) plus 3 m. pl. impf. qal of ידע (know), one of six *pe-yodh* verbs like יֵשֵׁב.

הסבת. 2 m. s. pf. hiphil of double-*ayin* verb סבב (turn about).

לבם. Masc. noun לֵב (alternative form to לֵבָב, heart) plus 3 m. pl. suffix. Root is double-*ayin*, hence *dagesh-forte* in *beth*.

אחרנית. Adverb, properly a fem. adj. form (backwards).

Verse 38. ותפל. Strong-*waw* plus 3 f. s. impf. qal of נפל (fall).

אש יהוה. LXX, Lucian and Targum have 'fire from the LORD', i.e. אש מֵאֵת־יהוה, but this is not necessary.

52

לחכה. 3 f. s. pf. piel of לחך (lick up), normally לְחֲכָה, but with tone retracted in pause, turning vocal *shewa* into original *tsere*, DG 40 (bottom), WL 117.

Verse 39. וירא. Strong-*waw* plus 3 m. s. impf. qal of ראה (see), special apocopated form, DG 147, WL 144.

ויפלו. Strong-*waw* plus 3 m. pl. impf. qal of נפל (fall).

פניהם. Plural noun פָּנִים (faces) plus 3 m. pl. suffix.

היא. 3 m. s. personal pronoun. This is the normal way of saying 'JHVH is the God' (DG 46), but the Hebrew probably carries more emphasis than this, WL 4, GK 145*u* (note 3, 'emphatically resuming the subject').

Verse 40. תפשו. 2 m. pl. imperat. qal of תפש (lay hold).

אַל with the jussive is usually a mild prohibition: see note on 17¹³.

ימלט. 3 m. s. impf. niphal of מלט (escape, deliver).

מהם. Prep. *min* (*tsere* before consonant which cannot be doubled) plus 3 m. pl. suffix, DG 53, WL 110f.

ויתפשום. Strong-*waw* plus 3 m. pl. impf. qal of תפש (lay hold) plus 3 m. pl. suffix.

וירדם. Strong-*waw* plus 3 m. s. impf. hiphil of ירד (go down) plus 3 m. pl. suffix.

וישחטם. Strong-*waw* plus 3 m. s. impf. qal of שחט (slaughter) plus 3 m. pl. suffix.

53

Verse 41. עלה. 2 m. s. imperat. qal of עלה (go up), followed by similar forms of אכל (eat) and (with *waw*-copula, -*u* before *shewa*) of שתה (drink).

קול המון. Two cstr. sing. nouns, 'the sound of the roar (absolute is הָמוֹן) of the rains'.

הגשם. Article plus גֶּשֶׁם (*qamets* for *seghol* in pause with *silluq*, DG 40, WL 117), the seasonal downpour, either the former (Oct.–Nov.) or the latter (March–April) rains.

Verse 42. ויעלה. Strong-*waw* plus 3 m. s. impf. qal (*not* apoc.) of עלה (go up).

לאכל. Prep. *lamedh* plus inf. cstr. qal of אכל (eat), pattern of -*es* completed before *chateph-seghol*, followed by similar form (with *waw*-copula) of שתה (drink).

ויגהר. Strong-*waw* plus 3 m. s. impf. qal of גהר (crouch), only here and 2 Kings 4³⁴*f.*

ארצה. Fem. noun אֶרֶץ (earth) plus *he-locale* (of direction towards); the *he* does not take the tone, DG 61, WL 55 and 211.

בֵּין. Prep. 'between'.

ברכו. The Qere is בִּרְכָּיו, 3 m. s. suffix to dual of בֶּרֶךְ (knee). Duals have singular stem with plural suffixes, though this shows only in segholates and in feminine nouns generally, DG 69 and 101, WL 64 and 95.

Verse 43. נערו. 3 m. s. suffix to sing. of masc. noun נַעַר (youth).

54

הבט. 2 m. s. imperat. hiphil of נבט (look), found only in piel and hiphil.

ויעל. Strong-*waw* plus 3 m. s. impf. qal (apoc.) of עלה (go up).

ויבט. Strong-*waw* plus 3 m. s. impf. hiphil of נבט (look).

אין מאומה, 'nothing of anything'.

שב. 2 m. s. imperat. qal of שוב (return).

פעמים. Plural of פַּעַם (foot, time). LXX adds 'and the lad returned seven times', which is probably correct. The καὶ σύ of LXX (as if before שב, return) may be due to reading וְאַתָּה (and thou) for an original וְעַתָּה (and now), cf. the reading of Codex Vaticanus.

Verse 44. בשביעית. Prep. *beth* plus article plus ordinal numeral 'seventh', DG 165, WL 197.

עב. Masc. (but here fem.) noun, meaning 'cloud'. The root is *ayin-waw* עוב (be hidden), so that cstr. pl. is עָבֵי with firm *qamets*.

קטנה. Fem. sing. of adj. קָטָן (small). The original *pathach* is retained with suffices, hence the *dagesh* in the *nun*, DG 141, WL 55, GK 93*ee*.

ככף. Prep. *kaph* plus cstr. sing. of כַּף (hollow of hand, foot) a double-*ayin* root.

עלה. Fem. sing. (note the *qamets*) of act. ptc. qal of עלה (go up).

מים. Prep. *min* plus יָם (sea), with *qamets* for *pathach* in pause with *athnach*, DG 40, WL 117.

אֱסֹר. 2 m. s. imperat. qal of אסר (bind), here of saddling horse.

וָרֵד. Waw-copula (qamets in pretone in pair, DG 53, WL 45) plus 2 m. s. imperat. qal of ירד (go down).

יַעְצָרְכָה. 3 m. s. impf. qal of עצר (withhold, restrain) plus 2 m. s. suffix with qamets written full, 'and the downpour will not hold you up'.

Verse 45. עַד־כֹּה וְעַד־כֹּה, idiomatic for 'in quite a short time'.

הִתְקַדְּרוּ. 3 m. pl. pf. hithpael of קדר (be black).
עָבִים. Plural of masc. noun עָב (cloud).

וַיִּרְכַּב. Strong-waw plus 3 m. s. impf. qal of רכב (mount and ride).

יִזְרְעֶאלָה. He-locale (toneless, DG 61, WL 55 and 211) plus place name.

אֶל instead of expected עַל, as often.

וַיְשַׁנֵּס. Strong-waw (dagesh fails in yodh-with-shewa) plus 3 m. s. impf. piel of שנס, verb not known, but there is an Aramaic verb שְׁנַץ, used of binding up sandals, whence it is thought that the meaning is 'gird up'.

מָתְנָיו. Dual plus 3 m. s. suffix, 'his loins': short-o in the first (closed) syllable.

וַיָּרָץ. Pronounce wăy-yā́-rŏts: strong-waw plus 3 m. s. impf. qal of רוץ (run).

בֹּאֲכָה. Inf. cstr. qal of בּוֹא (come) plus 2 m. s. suffix with qamets written full.

CHAPTER XIX

Verse 1. וַיַּגֵּד. Strong-*waw* plus 3 m. s. impf. hiphil of נגד (tell).

וְאֵת כָּל אֲשֶׁר. 'And all that he had slain . . .', but LXX presupposes the omission of כל, and so all Versions except Targum. Commentators generally favour this omission, but MT is not as barbarous as they suppose. In each case אֲשֶׁר is used as a relative conjunction introducing a clause.

בֶּחָרֶב. Prep. *beth* plus article plus pausal form of fem. noun חֶרֶב (sword). Normal form is בַּחֶרֶב, but the first *seghol* has become *qamets* in pause, so that vowel of article is now *seghol*, DG 44, WL 27.

Verse 2. וַתִּשְׁלַח. Strong-*waw* plus 3 f. s. impf. qal of שלח (send).

מַלְאָךְ. Masculine noun (messenger).

כֹּה יַעֲשֹׂוּן . . . Regular form of oath found in Samuel and Kings: lit. 'So may the gods do (to me: so the Versions here) and so may they add', with the verbs in the sing. when a Hebrew is swearing by the Hebrew God. In LXX and Lucian here, the oath is prefixed by אִם אַתָּה אֵלִיָּהוּ וַאֲנִי אִיזֶבֶל 'as surely as you are Elijah and I am Jezebel', which bears every evidence of being original.

יַעֲשֹׂוּן. 3 m. pl. impf. qal of עשׂה (do). The final *nun* is added for effect, but it is a false archaism, belonging

57

to the 2nd person only, DG 77, WL 77 and especially
GK 47*m*.

יוספון. 3 m. pl. impf. hiphil of יסף (add), with same
archaic *nun*.

כעת. Prep. *kaph* plus article plus fem. (occasionally
masc.) noun (time), 'about the (this) time', found
eight times, of which five are in Kings.

מחר. Noun (the morrow), often used as adverb.
The root מהר with *he* means hurry.

אשים. 1 s. impf. qal of שׂים (set).

נפשך. 2 m. s. suffix to sing. of fem. noun נֶפֶשׁ (life,
self).

אַחַד. Cstr. sing. (before prep. *min*) of ordinal 'one'.
The masc. absolute is אֶחָד, DS 50 (§35, Rem. 2). GK
130*g* denies that we have a construct form here, making
it 'merely a rhythmical shortening of the usual (tone-
lengthened) form'.

Verse 3. וַיַּרְא. Strong-*waw* plus 3 m. s. impf. (apoc.) qal
of ראה (see), DG 147, WL 144. All the Versions, except
Targum, read וַיִּרָא, strong-*waw* plus 3 m. s. impf. qal
of יָרֵא (be afraid), usually written יִּירָא. This is un-
doubtedly correct.

ויקם. See note on 17¹⁰.

וילך. See note on 17⁵.

58

אל־נפשׁו, 'for his life'. The prep. עַל is found in Gen. 19¹⁷.

ויבא. Strong-*waw* plus 3 m. s. impf. qal of בּוֹא (come).

ליהודה. Prep. *lamedh* (long-*i* without *shewa* before *yodh*-with-*shewa*, DG 51, WL 43) plus יְהוּדָה.

וינח. Strong-*waw* plus 3 m. s. impf. 2nd hiphil of נוּחַ (rest). This *ayin-waw* verb has two hiphils. The true hiphil has pf. הֵנִיחַ and impf. יָנִיחַ, and means 'cause to rest'. The 2nd hiphil has pf. הִנִּיחַ and impf. יַנִּיחַ, and means 'deposit, leave'.

Verse 4. The והוא is emphatic, 'but *he* . . .'.

במדבר. Prep. *beth* plus article plus מִדְבָּר (wilderness).

וישׁב. See note on 17⁵.

רתם אחת, 'a certain broom-bush'. The noun is masc. (cf. verse 5), so that the Qere is correcting the gender of the numeral 'one' to the masc. אֶחָד. This use of אחד following a noun without the article and meaning 'a certain' is characteristic of these Northern narratives which have been added to the original Book of Kings.

וישׁאל. Strong-*waw* plus 3 m. s. impf. qal of שׁאל (ask).

את־נפשׁו. This might be a loose accusative, 'in respect of his life (breath-soul, himself) to die', but Ewald and perhaps GK 157c explain it as an accusative and infinitive construction (cf. Latin) after a verb of asking.

59

למות. Prep. *lamedh* (*qamets* in pretone before inf. cstr., DG 51, WL 45) plus inf. cstr. qal of מות (die). Note the *-u*. The form with *-o* is either inf. abs. qal of the verb or cstr. sing. of the noun מָוֶת (death).

רב. Masc. adj. used as interjection 'enough'.

קח. 2 m. s. imperat. qal of לקח (take away), DG 213, WL 255.

טוב מן. Masc. adj. טוב (good) plus *min*-comparative, DG 161, WL 31f, GK 133*a*.

מאבתי. Prep. *min* (*tsere* before consonant which cannot be doubled, DG 52, WL 32) plus pl. of אָב (father, DG 153, WL 185) plus 1 sing. suffix, with *qamets* for *pathach* in pause, DG 40, WL 117.

Verse 5. וישכב. Strong-*waw* plus 3 m. s. impf. qal of שכב (lie down).

ויישן. Strong-*waw* plus 3 m. s. impf. qal of יָשֵׁן (sleep): ordinary *pe-yodh* form. LXX follows with ἐκεῖ, whilst Lucian has it later, after the phrase תחת רתם אחד. Probably the original text read שָׁם (there), and the other phrase has been repeated from verse 4.

זה. Enclitic, emphasising 'behold', DS 5, GK 136*c*.

נגע. Masc. sing. act. ptc. of נגע (touch), followed by prep. *beth* instead of by direct object.

קום. 2 m. s. imperat. qal of קוּם (arise), followed by similar form of אכל (eat), but with *waw* written full (one of five cases).

60

Verse 6. ויבט. See note on 18⁴³.

מראשתיו. 3 m. s. suffix to fem. plural noun מְרַאֲשֹׁת, 'the places near the head', and so 'at his head'.

עגת. Cstr. sing. of fem. noun עֻגָה (disc, round loaf of bread). The -*u* is long, and there should be no *dagesh* in the *gimel*, cf. 17¹³.

רצפים. Plural of fem. noun רִצְפָּה (glowing stone, coal).

צפחת. Cstr. sing. (same form) of צַפַּחַת (wide, broad jar), cf. 17¹².

וישׁת. Strong-*waw* plus 3 m. s. impf. (apoc.) qal of שׁתה (drink). This unusual apocopation is found also in וַיֵּבְךְּ, DG 147, WL 144.

וישׁב. Strong-*waw* plus 3 m. s. impf. qal of שׁוּב (return). True impf. is יָשׁוּב; jussive is יָשֹׁב, which with tone retracted (as here) becomes *wăy-yắ-shŏbh*. Idiomatic for 'he again lay down', WL 160, GK 120g.

וישׁכב. Strong-*waw* plus 3 m. s. impf. qal of שׁכב (lie down), but with *pathach* lengthened to *qamets* in pause with *silluq*.

מלאך. Cstr. sing. of masc. noun מַלְאָךְ (angel).

שׁנית. Ordinal numeral 'second'.

ויגע. Strong-*waw* plus 3 m. s. impf. qal of נגע (touch).

ממך. Prep. *min* plus 2 m. s. suffix (DG 53, WL 110f); 'too much for thee'.

61

הדרך. Article plus דֶּרֶךְ (way, journey) with *qamets*
for *seghol* in pause with *silluq*, DG 40, WL 117.

Verse 8. וישתה. Strong-*waw* plus 3 m. s. impf. qal (not
apocopated, as in previous verse, because of the pause)
of שתה (drink).

בכח. Prep. *beth* plus cstr. sing. (same form) of masc.
noun כֹּחַ (strength).

האכילה. Article plus fem. noun אֲכִילָה (food), form
found only here.

ארבעים. Cardinal numeral (forty), followed by noun
in singular, DG 163, WL 194.

Verse 9. המערה. See note on 18[4]. For use of article,
DS 26, GK 126*d*.

וילן. Strong-*waw* plus 3 m. s. impf. qal of לִין or לוּן
(lodge, spend the night).

מה. Interrogative (what?). See note on 17[18].

Verse 10. קנא. Inf. abs. piel of קנא (to be jealous, zealous),
followed by 1 s. pf. piel of same root. The inf. abs. is
placed thus before a finite form of the same verb for
emphasis, DG 77 (bottom), WL 101, DS 117, GK 113*n*.

צבאות. Plural of masc. noun צָבָא (host).

עזבו. 3 m. pl. pf. qal of עזב (forsake).

בריתך. 2 m. s. suffix to sing. of fem. noun בְּרִית
(covenant)

מזבחתיך. 2 m. s. suffix to plural of מִזְבֵּחַ (altar).

62

הרסו. 3 m. pl. pf. qal of הרס (throw down), normally הָרְסוּ, but with tone retracted on to the previous vocal-shewa, and original qamets appearing (DG 41, WL 117) in pause with zaqeph-qaton.

נביאיך. 2 m. pl. suffix to plural of נָבִיא (prophet).

הרגו. 3 pl. pf. qal of הרג (kill).

ואותר. Strong-waw plus 1 s. impf. niphal of יתר (remain over).

ויבקשו. Strong-waw plus 3 m. pl. impf. piel of בקש (seek), with dagesh-forte failing in both yodh and qoph with vocal shewa, DG 32, WL 20: 'and they have sought'.

לקחתה. Prep. lamedh plus inf. cstr. qal (קַחַת: the lamedh does not belong to the root) of לקח (take away) plus 3 f. s. suffix, DG 213, WL 255.

Verse 11. צא. 2 m. s. imperat. qal of יצא (go out), one of six pe-yodh verbs like יֵשֵׁב.

ועמדת. Strong-waw plus 2 m. s. pf. qal of עמד (stand). The accent is moved on to the last syllable, DG 86, WL 90 note. The form is consecutive from the previous imperative, and can be translated as such, DS 81 (§55 a), GK 112r.

בהר. Prep. beth plus article plus הַר (mountain): qamets before he-with-qamets-and-tone, DG 44, WL 27. Narrative resumes with והנה.

עבר. Act. ptc. qal of עבר (pass across). The scene is described as a present event, vividly.

63

רוּחַ. This fem. noun (wind) is followed by a fem. adj. (masc. גָּדוֹל, great), but the more remote adj. חָזָק (strong) has relapsed into masc., DS 47, GK 132d. Cf. Jer. 20⁹, Ezek. 2⁹. The following participles are also in masc. Some would make the first adj. masc., and thus reckon רוּחַ to be masc. here, as apparently in Exod. 10¹³.

מְפָרֵק. Masc. sing. ptc. piel of פרק (tear apart).

הָרִים. Plural of הַר (mountain), DG 45f, WL 27.

וּמְשַׁבֵּר. Waw-copula (-u before labial) plus m. s. ptc. piel of שׁבר (break).

סְלָעִים. Plural of masc. noun סֶלַע (crag).

וְאַחַר. Waw-copula plus prep. אַחַר (after).

רַעַשׁ. Masc. noun 'shaking', especially of an earth-quake.

Verse 12. קוֹל דְּמָמָה דַקָּה, 'the sound of a crushed silence'.

דַקָּה. Fem. s. of דַּק (thin, small, fine), from a double-ayin root (crush, thresh). Hence dagesh-forte in the qoph.

Verse 13. כִּשְׁמֹעַ. Prep. kaph plus inf. cstr. qal of שׁמע (hear): 'when Elijah heard'.

וַיָּלֶט. Strong-waw plus 3 m. s. impf. hiphil of לוּט (enwrap).

בְּאַדַּרְתּוֹ. Prep. beth plus sing. of fem. noun אַדֶּרֶת (mantle) plus 3 m. s. suffix. Root means 'wide, great' and thence 'glorious, majestic', so that the noun can mean 'magnificence' and also 'mantle', both splendid (Josh. 7²¹) and very ordinary (prophet's).

ויצא. Strong-*waw* plus 3 m. s. impf. qal of יצא (go out), one of six *pe-yodh* verbs like יֵשֵׁב.

ויעמד. Strong-*waw* plus 3 m. s. impf. qal of עמד (stand).

פתח. Cstr. sing. (same form) of masc. noun פֶּתַח (opening, door).

Verse 15. צֵא. 2 m. s. imperat. qal of יצא (go), followed by similar form of שׁוּב (return). See note on 17³.

לדרכך. Prep. *lamedh* plus noun דֶּרֶךְ (way, road) plus 2 m. s. suffix.

מדברה. Cstr. sing. (מִדְבַּר) of noun מִדְבָּר (wilderness) plus toneless *he-locale*, DG 61, WL 211, GK 90c.

ובאת. Strong-*waw* plus 2 m. s. pf. qal of בּוֹא (come), consecutive from an imperative (DS 81, GK 112r), followed by similar form of משׁח (anoint).

Verse 16. ותמשׁח. 2 m. s. impf. qal of משׁח (anoint).

תחתיך. Prep. תַּחַת (under, instead of) plus 2 m. s. suffix, apparently a dual form.

Verse 17. והיה. Strong-*waw* plus 3 m. s. pf. qal: see note on 17⁴.

הנמלט. Article plus m. s. participle niphal of מלט (escape). The participle ends in *qamets*; the perfect in *pathach*.

מחרב. Prep. *min* (*tsere* before consonant which cannot be doubled) plus cstr. sing. (same form) of fem. noun חֶרֶב (sword).

יָמִית. 3 m. s. impf. hiphil of מוּת (die).

Verse 18. וְהִשְׁאַרְתִּי. Strong-*waw* plus 1 s. pf. hiphil of שׁאר (leave over): 'and I shall leave'. LXX has 2 person sing.

שִׁבְעַת אֲלָפִים. 'Seven thousands'. Hebrew has two ways of saying 'seven thousands': שֶׁבַע אֶלֶף, which follows the rules in note on 17¹², אֶלֶף is masc. without article and therefore 'seven' is feminine absolute, whilst אֶלֶף is singular; and שִׁבְעַת אֲלָפִים, as here, where אֲלָפִים is plural, and the 'seven' is in the construct, though feminine.

הברכים. Article plus dual of fem. noun בֶּרֶךְ (knee).

כרעו. 3 pl. pf. qal of כרע (bow down).

הפה. Article plus masc. noun פֶּה (mouth), DG 153, WL 186.

נשק with a *qoph* is 'kiss', but נשׁך with a *kaph* is 'bite'.

Verse 19. וימצא. Strong-*waw* plus 3 m. s. impf. qal of מצא (find).

חרש. Act. ptc. qal of חרש I (cut in, engrave, plough).

שנים עשר (twelve), DG 164, WL 196. The construct שְׁנֵי is more usual.

צמדים. Plural of masc. noun צֶמֶד (pair, yoke).

וַיִּשְׁלִךְ. Strong-*waw* plus 3 m. s. impf. hiphil of שׁלךְ (cast).

Verse 20. וַיַּעֲזֹב. Strong-*waw* plus 3 m. s. impf. qal of עזב (forsake).

הַבָּקָר. Article plus collective noun בָּקָר (cattle).

אֶשְּׁקָה. 1 sing. impf. (cohortative) qal of נשׁק (kiss). Some texts have *chaṭeph-qamets-chaṭuph* ('baby-*o*') under the *shin*.

לְאָבִי. Prep. *lamedh* plus noun אָב (father, DG 153, WL 185) plus 1 sing. suffix, followed by similar form of אֵם (mother), double-*ayin* root.

וְאֵלְכָה. Weak-*waw* plus 1 s. impf. (cohortative) qal of הלךְ (go).

אַחֲרֶיךָ. Prep. אַחֲרֵי (after) plus 2 m. s. suffix.

לָךְ. Prep. *lamedh* plus 2 m. s. suffix pausal form. Normal is לְךָ, DG 51, WL 49.

Verse 21. מֵאַחֲרָיו. Prep. *min* (*tsere* before *aleph*, cannot be doubled) plus prep. אַחֲרֵי (after) plus 3 sing. suffix.

וַיִּקַּח. See note on 17²³.

וַיִּזְבָּחֵהוּ. Strong-*waw* plus 3 m. s. impf. qal of זבח (slaughter) plus 3 m. s. suffix.

וּבִכְלִי. *Waw*-copula (-*u* before labial) plus prep. *beth* plus cstr. pl. of כְּלִי (vessel, instrument), DG 153, WL 186.

67

בִּשְּׁלָם. 3 m. s. pf. piel of בָּשַׁל (boil) plus 3 m. pl. suffix.

וַיִּתֵּן. Strong-*waw* plus 3 m. s. impf. qal of נָתַן (give), DG 213, WL 255.

לָעָם. Prep. *lamedh* plus article plus עַם (people), DG 45, WL 27.

וַיֹּאכְלוּ. Strong-*waw* plus 3 m. pl. impf. qal of אָכַל (eat), with tone retracted in pause and original *tsere* returning, DG 41, WL 117.

וַיְשָׁרְתֵהוּ. Strong-*waw* plus 3 m. s. impf. piel of שָׁרַת (minister, serve) plus 3 m. s. suffix. *Dagesh* fails in *yodh*-with-*shewa* (DG 32, WL 20), and *resh* cannot be doubled.

נחלת. Cstr. sing. of fem. noun נַחֲלָה (inheritance).

אבתי. 1 s. suffix to plural of אָב (father), DG 153, WL 185.

לָךְ. Pausal form of לְךָ: see note 19²⁰.

Verse 4. ויבא. See note on 17¹⁰.

סַר. Adjective (sullen, stubborn), double-*ayin* root, so that cstr. plural is סָרֵי.

זעף. Adjective (out of humour).

אתן. 1 s. impf. qal of נתן (give), DG 213, WL 255.

אבותי. 1 s. suffix (*qamets* for *pathach* in pause with *athnach*) to plural of אָב (father).

מטתו. 3 m. s. suffix to singular of fem. noun מִטָּה (couch, bed).

ויסב. Strong-*waw* plus 3 m. s. impf. hiphil of סבב (turn around). LXX and Lucian have καὶ συνεκάλυφεν, reading וַיְכַס, strong-*waw* plus 3 m. s. impf. (apoc.) piel of כסה (cover).

Verse 5. ותבא. Strong-*waw* plus 3 f. s. impf. qal of בּוֹא (come).

אשתו. 3 m. s. suffix to fem. noun אִשָּׁה (woman, wife), DG 153, WL 185.

ותדבר. Strong-*waw* plus 3 f. s. impf. piel of דִּבֶּר (speak).

71

זה. Here enclitic, 'why on earth is thy spirit sullen . . . ', DS 7, GK 136c.

סרה. Fem. sing. of adjective סַר (sullen), double-*ayin* root.

ואינך. *Waw*-copula plus אַיִן (nothingness) plus 2 m. s. suffix, 'and (why) are you not eating bread?'

Verse 6. כי introducing direct speech, DS 197 Rem. 2, GK 157b.

אדבר. 1 s. impf. qal of דִּבֵּר (speak), 'I was speaking.'

ואמר. Strong-*waw* plus 1 s. impf. qal of אמר (say), *pe-aleph* verb.

בכסף. *Beth* of price, DS 139 (near bottom), GK 119p.

תחתיו. See note on 21².

Verse 7. A question begins with אתה, and ends at the *athnach*. It is not necessary always to have the inter-rogative particle, DS 166, GK 150a. Presumably the question is indicated by the tone of the voice.

מלוכה. Fem. noun (kingship, royalty).

קום. See note on 19⁵.

אֱכָל־. 2 m. s. imperat. qal of אכל (eat), but with short-*o* because of following *maqqeph*, DG 40, WL 28.

וְיִטַב. Weak-*waw* plus 3 m. s. impf. qal of יטב (to be good), a true *pe-yodh* which always retains the radical-*yodh*, cf. ילל (howl) and ינק (suck). This form is usually written וְיִיטַב: 'and let thy heart be good'.

לבך. Noun לֵב (heart); double-*ayin* root, hence *dagesh* in *beth*; plus 2 m. s. suffix, but with tone retracted in pause with *zaqeph-qaton*, so that the vocal *shewa* becomes *seghol*, DG 41, WL 117, GK 29n.

The אני (I) is emphatic: '*I* will give you . . .'

Verse 8. **ותכתב.** Strong-*waw* plus 3 f. s. impf. qal of כתב (write): 'so she wrote . . .'

ספרים. Plural of masc. noun סֵפֶר (missive, scroll, book).

בשם. Perp. *beth* plus cstr. sing. of masc. noun שֵׁם (name).

ותחתם. Strong-*waw* plus 3 f. s. impf. qal of חתם (seal).

בחתמו. Prep. *beth* plus masc. noun חֹתָם (seal) plus 3 m. s. suffix.

ותשלח. Strong-*waw* plus 3 f. s. impf. qal of שלח (send).

הספרים. The Masoretes preferred to omit the article (so the Qere), but it is better to read the Kethib הַסְּפָרִים (the letters).

הזקנים. Article plus plural of זָקֵן (beard, old man).

החרים. Article plus plural of חֹר (noble), a Northern word from חרר II (be free).

אשר בעירו, 'who were in his city', omitted by LXX and Lucian because they took the following phrase to

73

mean 'those who dwelt with Naboth'; cf. Syriac 'who dwelt in the city with Naboth'. But הַיֹּשְׁבִים (article plus m. pl. act. ptc. qal of ישׁב) means 'those who sat in council'.

Verse 9. בַּסְּפָרִים. Prep. *beth* plus article plus pl. of סֵפֶר (letter).

קִרְאוּ. 2 m. pl. imperat. qal of קרא I (call).

צוֹם. Masculine noun (fast).

וְהוֹשִׁיבוּ. Weak-*waw* (copula) plus 2 m. pl. imperat. hiphil of ישׁב (sit).

Verse 10. שְׁנָיִם. Cardinal numeral 'two': before a masc. noun, and so in absolute and agreeing in gender, see note on 17¹².

אֲנָשִׁים. Plural of אִישׁ (man), DG 153, WL 255.

בְּנֵי. Cstr. pl. of בֵּן (son), DG 153, WL 186. 'Sons of Belial' are sons of בְּלִי (not) יַעַל (profit), i.e. sons of no-good. But see Burney, p. 245.

נֶגְדוֹ. 3 m. s. suffix to noun נֶגֶד (what is conspicuous, in front of), used as prep. (as here) or as adverb (opposite him).

וִיעִדֻהוּ. Weak-*waw* plus 3 m. pl. impf. hiphil of עוּד, denominative verb meaning 'give witness (עֵד)', plus 3 m. s. suffix: 'and let them give witness against him', with direct accusative.

בֵּרַכְתָּ. 2 m. s. pf. piel of ברך (bless), euphemism deliberately substituted.

וּמֶלֶךְ. *Waw*-copula (*qamets* before tone in a pair, DG 53, WL 44) plus noun מֶלֶךְ (king).

וְהוֹצִיאֻהוּ. Weak-*waw* (copula) plus 2 m. pl. imperat. hiphil of יצא (go out) plus 3 m. s. suffix.

וּסְקָלֻהוּ. *Waw*-copula plus 2 m. pl. imperat. qal of סקל (stone) plus 3 m. sing. suffix.

וְיָמֹת. Weak-*waw* (*īva*-clause) plus 3 m. s. impf. (jussive) qal of מות (die).

Verse 11. וַיַּעֲשׂוּ. See note on 18²⁶.

שָׁלְחָה. 3 f. s. pf. qal of שלח (send). Translate as pluperfect, DS 58 (bottom), GK 106*f*.

כַּאֲשֶׁר כָּתוּב. Lucian omits to end of sentence, probably rightly, because it is redundant.

כָּתוּב. Masc. sing. pass. ptc. qal of כתב (write).

Verse 12. וְהֵשִׁיבוּ. We should expect this to be וַיּוֹשִׁיבוּ, strong-*waw* plus 3 m. pl. impf. hiphil of ישב (sit). Probably an error due to the previous imperat. hiphil, and not intended for pf. hiphil with weak-*waw*.

Verse 13. וַיֵּשְׁבוּ. Strong-*waw* plus 3 m. pl. impf. qal of ישב (sit).

וַיְעִדֻהוּ. Strong-*waw* plus 3 m. pl. impf. hiphil of עוד (testify, give witness) plus 3 m. s. suffix. Cf. verse 10.

בֵּרַךְ. 3 m. s. pf. piel of ברך (bless); *tsere* because the *resh* cannot be doubled. The *pathach*, which occurs for

75

tsere occasionally in the regular verb, is more frequent in *ayin*-guttural verbs, GK 64*c*.

ויצִאֻהוּ. Strong-*waw* plus 3 m. pl. impf. hiphil of יצא (go out) plus 3 m. s. suffix. The form occurs three times, in two of which neither the hiphil-*i* nor the final -*u* of the impf. pl. are written.

מִחוּץ לְ. Prep. *min* plus masc. noun חוּץ (the outside), followed by prep. *lamedh*.

וַיִסְקְלֻהוּ. Strong-*waw* plus 3 m. pl. impf. qal of סקל (stone) plus 3 m. s. suffix.

בָּאֲבָנִים. Prep. *beth* plus article plus pl. of masc. noun אֶבֶן (stone). For use of article (where we would not use it) DS 26, GK 126*d*.

וַיָּמֹת. Strong-*waw* plus 3 m. s. impf. (jussive form with strong-*waw*) qal of מוּת (die). Tone not retracted because in pause at end of verse.

Verse 15. כִּשְׁמֹעַ. Prep. *kaph* plus inf. cstr. qal of שמע (hear).

סֻקַּל. 3 m. s. pf. pual of סקל (stone), pluperfect.

וַיָּמֹת. Strong-*waw* plus 3 m. s. impf. (jussive form) qal of מוּת (die), 'and had died'. Tone not retracted, because at end of clause (with *athnach*).

רֵשׁ. 2 m. s. imperat. qal of ירשׁ (inherit, possess).

מֵאֵן. 3 m. s. pf. piel of מאן (refuse).

לָתֵת-. Prep. *lamedh* (*qamets* before an inf. cstr., DG 51, WL 45), plus inf. cstr. qal (תֵּת) of נתן (give), but

76

with *tsere* shortened to *seghol* before *maqqeph*, DG 40, WL 28.

חי. Adjective (alive).

מֵת. This form may be 3 m. s. pf. qal or act. ptc. qal of מוּת (die). Since it is preceded by כי, it is probably the perfect: 'for he had died'. About ten Hebrew MSS. have כי אם, which is good Hebrew for 'but, except' after a negative. In this case the translation is: 'for Naboth is not alive, but dead'.

Verse 16. מת is definitely the perfect qal here.

ויקם. See note on 17¹⁰.

לרדת. Prep. *lamedh* (*qamets* before an inf. cstr., DG 51, WL 45) plus inf. cstr. qal of ירד (go down).

לרשתו. Prep. *lamedh* plus inf. cstr. qal (רֶשֶׁת) of ירש (possess) plus 3 m. s. suffix.

Verse 18. רד. 2 m. s. imperat. qal of ירד (go down).

לקראת. See note on 18¹⁶.

Verse 19. ודברת. Strong-*waw* plus 2 m. s. pf. piel of דבר (speak), with tone moved on to the last syllable, DG 86, WL 90 note.

הרצחת. Interrogative-*he* (DG 167, WL 28f) plus 2 m. s. pf. qal of רצח (murder).

ירשת. 2 m. s. pf. qal of ירש (possess), with *qamets* for *pathach* in pause with *athnach*, DG 40, WL 117.

77

במקום. Prep. *beth* plus cstr. sing. of masc. noun מָקוֹם (place). The construct precedes the clause which is introduced by אֲשֶׁר, DS 35, GK 130c. This is comparatively common with מקום.

לקקו. 3 pl. pf. qal of לקק (lick).

הכלבים. Article plus plural of masc. noun כֶּלֶב (dog).

דם. Cstr. sing. of masc. noun דָם (blood). Usually the plural is used of shed blood.

ילקו. 3 m. pl. impf. qal of double-*ayin* verb לקק (lick, lap).

דמך. 2 m. s. suffix to sing. דם (blood).

גם־אתה. This is the way in which a suffix is emphasised, i.e. the particle גַּ (also) with the appropriate pronoun, here אַתָּה 2nd masc. sing., DS 1, GK 135g. Here the *pathach* of the tone-syllable has become *qamets* in pause with *silluq*, DG 40, WL 117.

Verse 20. המצאתני. Interrogative-*he* (DG 167, WL 28f) plus 2 m. s. pf. qal (מָצָאתָ) of מצא (find) plus 1 s. suffix. Note that the vowel under the *tau* is *pathach*, and definitely not *qamets*, which is wrong except in pause.

איבי. 1 s. suffix to singular אוֹיֵב (enemy). Here a vocative.

יען. Properly a noun meaning 'intention', but used as prep. or conjunction 'because'. Here prep. with inf. cstr.

78

התמכרך. Inf. cstr. hithpael of מכר (sell) plus 2 m. s. suffix. LXX and Lucian add μάτην (in vain) i.e. לַשָּׁוְא.

לעשות. Prep. *lamedh* plus inf. cstr. qal of עשה (do).

הרע. Article plus masc. noun רַע (evil), double-*ayin* root. At end of verse LXX and Lucian add (Lucian τοῦ) παροργίσαι αὐτόν, i.e. לְהַכְעִיסוֹ, prep. *lamedh* plus inf. cstr. hiphil of כעס (be jealous, vexed) plus 3 m. s. suffix. Probably a scribe influenced by his memory of other passages.

Verse 21. הנני. Demonstrative article הִנֵּה (behold) plus 1 s. suffix, DG 142 note (but 'behold he' is regularly הִנֵּה הוּא), WL 110f, GK 100*o* and 147*b*.

מבי. The *aleph* has been dropped by error. The Qere is מֵבִיא, hiphil ptc. of בוא (come), 'behold I am about to bring', future *instans*, DS 134, GK 116*p*, DT 168.

רעה. Fem. noun (evil). The root is double-*ayin*, so first *qamets* is firm.

ובערתי. Strong-*waw* (-*u* before labial) plus 1 s. pf. piel of (burn, consume).

והכרתי. Strong-*waw* plus 1 s. pf. hiphil of כרת (cut, cut off). The *tau* of the ending has assimilated to the *tau* of the root.

לאחאב. Prep. *lamedh* (in respect of, so far as Ahab is concerned) plus proper name, WL 207 (top), DS 140, GK 143*e*.

מַשְׁתִּין. Hiphil ptc. of a form שָׁתַן, secondary root from שִׁין (urinate).

בְקִיר. Prep. *beth* plus masc. noun קִיר (wall).

עָצוּר וְעָזוּב. Two passive qal participles, 'restrained and let loose'. The phrase is found thrice in Deuteronomic sources in Kings and also in Deut. 32³⁶. The most satisfactory explanation is that of Ewald, 'kept in through ritual defilement and at large', but see note in Burney, p. 186.

Verse 22. וְנָתַתִּי. Strong-*waw* plus 1 s. pf. qal of נתן (give, set), DG 213, WL 255.

אֶל־הַכַּעַס. Prep. אֶל (to) instead of prep. עַל (on account of).

הַכַּעַס. Article plus masc. noun כַּעַס (vexation, anger).

הִכְעַסְתָּ. 2 m. s. pf. hiphil of כעס (vex).

וַתַּחֲטִא. Strong-*waw* plus 2 m. s. impf. hiphil of חטא (sin), one of a number of cases with -*i* in the final syllable instead of the normal *tsere*, GK 74*l*.

Verse 23. לְאִיזֶבֶל. Prep. *lamedh* (in respect of) plus proper name.

יֹאכְלוּ. 3 m. pl. impf. qal of אכל (eat), *pe-aleph* verb.

בְחֵל. Prep. *beth* plus cstr. sing. (same form) of masc. noun חֵל (rampart); so LXX and Lucian, but Vulgate, Syriac and Targum read בְּחֵלֶק (in the portion of, field of), which may well be original.

Verse 24. הַמֵּת. Article plus act. ptc. qal of מוּת (die), i.e. 'the dead belonging to Ahab'.

כַּשָּׂדֶה. Prep. *beth* plus article plus שָׂדֶה (field), strictly 'the open country round the village, town'.

הַשָּׁמַיִם. Article plus שָׁמַיִם (heavens), with *qamets* for *pathach* in pause with *silluq*.

Verse 25. רַק. Adverb with restrictive force, a synonym of אַךְ, except that רק is used more often preceding a single word. Here 'howbeit'.

הִתְמַכֵּר. 3. m. s. pf. hithpael of מכר (sell).

הֵסַתָּה. This form is 3 f. s. pf. hiphil of a form סתת, but since it is intended to be from סוּת (incite, allure), it should be הֵסִיתָה. 'Whom Jezebel his wife incited.'

Verse 26. וַיַּתְעֵב. Strong-*waw* plus 3 m. s. impf. hiphil of תעב, denominative verb from noun תּוֹעֵבָה (abomination), here 'to do abominably' (in connection with idolatry and apostasy).

לָלֶכֶת. Prep. *lamedh* (*qamets* before an inf. cstr., DG 51, WL 45) plus inf. cstr. qal of הלך (go).

הַגִּלּוּלִים. Article plus plural of masc. noun גִּלּוּל (idol), found only in plural. The pronunciation is artificial, the word having been given the vowels of the word שִׁקּוּץ (detestable thing); cf. Amos 5²⁶ כִּיּוּן and סִכּוּת. The Aramaic word is גְּלָלָא, so that the true Hebrew pointing may have been גְּלָלִים (idol-stones).

Gesenius connected the word with גלל II (roll) and so 'idol-logs'. Jewish tradition connects with גֵּלֵל (dung).

ככל. Prep. *kaph* plus noun כל (all).

הוריש. 3 m. s. pf. hiphil of ירש (possess, dispossess).

Verse 27. ויקרע. Strong-*waw* plus 3 m. s. impf. qal of קרע (rend).

בגדיו. 3 m. s. suffix to plural of masc. noun בֶּגֶד (cloak, garment).

וַיָּשֶׂם־. Strong-*waw* plus 3 m. s. impf. (jussive form) qal of שִׂים (set), with *tsere* shortened into *seghol* before *maqqeph*.

שַׂק. An Egyptian loanword (sackcloth), which has come into English through Greek and Latin.

בשרו. 3 m. s. suffix to masc. noun בָּשָׂר (flesh).

ויצם. Strong-*waw* plus 3 m. s. impf. qal of צוּם (fast). Tone not retracted because of pause.

בַּשָּׂק. Prep. *beth* plus article plus שַׂק (sackcloth), with *pathach* lengthened to *qamets* in pause with *zaqeph-qaton*.

ויהלך. Strong-*waw* plus 3 m. s. impf. piel of הלך (walk).

אט. Noun (gentleness), used as adverb. Omitted by LXX and Lucian; Syriac and Targum have 'barefoot'; Vulgate 'with bowed head'.

Verse 29. הראית. Interrogative-*he* (DG 167, WL 28f) plus 2 m. s. pf. qal of ראה (see).

נכנע. 3 m. s. pf. niphal of כנע (be humble).

מלפני. Prep. *min* plus לְפְנֵי (prep. *lamedh* plus cstr. of פָּנִים, faces, but used a prep. 'before'), but with 1 sing. suffix, and with *qamets* for *pathach* in pause with *silluq*.

אבי. Error for אביא (so Qere): 1 s. impf. hiphil of בוֹא (come).

הרעה. Article plus fem. noun רָעָה (evil).

בימיו. Prep. *beth* plus 3 m. s. suffix to plural of יוֹם (day), DG 153, WL 186.

בימי. Prep. *beth* plus יְמֵי, cstr. pl. of יוֹם (day). *Shewa* fails under *yodh* preceded by half-open syllable with -*i*, DG 51, WL 43.

בנו. 3 m. s. suffix plus sing. בֵּן (son), DG 153, WL 185.

CHAPTER XXII

Verse 1. וישבו. From ישב (sit, dwell, tarry). See note on 21¹³.

שלש. Cardinal numeral (three), before fem. noun without article: therefore differs in gender, is in absolute, precedes noun: see 17¹².

שנים. Plural of fem. noun שנה (year).

Verse 2. השלישת. Article plus ordinal numeral (fem.) 'third'.

וירד. Strong-*waw* plus 3 m. s. impf. qal of ירד (go down), with tone retracted, and *tsere* reduced to *seghol* in last syllable.

Verse 3. עבדיו. 3 m. s. suffix to plural of עֶבֶד (servant).

הידעתם. Interrogative-*he* plus 2 m. pl. pf. qal of ידע (know).

לנו. Prep. *lamedh* plus 1 pl. suffix, DG 51, WL 49.

מחשים. Masc. pl. of hiphil ptc. of חשה (be inactive).

מקחת. Prep. *min* plus inf. cstr. qal of לקח (take), DG 213, WL 255.

אתה. Particle אֶת (marking definite accusative) plus 3 f. 2. suffix, DG 75, WL 49.

Verse 4. התלך. Interrogative-*he* plus 2 m. s. impf. qal of הלך (go).

אתי. Prep. אֶת (with) plus 1 sing. suffix, DG 142, WL 49.

למלחמה. Prep. *lamedh* plus article plus fem. noun מִלְחָמָה (battle, war), followed by place name.

כמוני כמוך. 'Like me, like thee'. Prep. *kaph* (form כְּמוֹ is used for light suffixes) plus 1 sing. and 2 masc. sing. suffixes, DG 87, WL 110f.

כעמי כעמך. Similar construction. Prep. *kaph* plus 1 s. suffix to sing. עַם (people), followed by *kaph* plus 2 m. s. suffix to sing. עם, but with tone retracted in pause with *tiphcha*, and *seghol* instead of vocal *shewa*, DG 41, WL 117, GK 29*n*.

Verse 5. דְרָשׁ־נָא. Pronounce *derosh-na*, with short-*o* because of *maqqeph*, DG 40, WL 28. 2 m. s. imperat. qal of דרשׁ (enquire), with particle of entreaty.

כיום. Prep. *kaph* plus article plus יוֹם (day), lit. 'about today', meaning 'now', or 'at once', 'first of all', which last is probably the meaning here.

Verse 6. ויקבץ. See note on 18[20].

אלהם. Prep. אֶל (to) plus 3 m. pl. suffix, DG 70, WL 64f; one of thirteen cases in the book where the *yodh* is not written.

האלך. Interrogative-*he* (part of a double question, the other element being introduced by אִם, DG 168, §48, 5c; WL 78) plus 1 s. impf. qal of הלך (go).

אחדל‎. 1 s. impf. qal of חדל‎ (cease, refrain), but with *qamets* for *pathach* in pause with *athnach*.

עלה‎. See note on 18⁴¹.

ויתן‎. Weak-*waw* plus 3 m. s. impf. qal of נתן‎ (give).

אדני‎. The actual word אדני‎ is written here instead of יהוה‎.

Verse 7. האין‎. Interrogative-*he* plus אֵין‎, cstr. of negative אַיִן‎, and used regularly as particle of negation: 'is there not?'

ונדרשה‎. Weak-*waw* plus 1 pl. impf. (cohortative) qal of דרש‎ (enquire), DG 83, WL 85f.

מאותו‎. Prep. *min* plus accusative particle אֶת‎ plus 3 m. s. suffix, but it ought to be מֵאִתּוֹ‎, prep. אֵת‎ (with) plus 3 m. s. suffix. For differences, see DG 75 (particle) and 142 (prep.); WL 49 (particle) and 49 (prep.). Similarly in next verse.

Verse 8. שנאתיו‎. 1 s. pf. qal of שָׂנֵא‎ (hate) plus 3 m. s. suffix.

יתנבא‎. 3 m. s. impf. hithpael of denominative verb נבא‎ (act as a נָבִיא‎, prophet); impf. of repeated action, DG 157, WL 67, DS 65, GK 107*e*.

עלי‎. Prep. עַל‎ (concerning) plus 1 s. suffix, DG 70, WL 64f.

כי אם‎. After a negative is 'except', DG 168, WL 111, DS 203, GK 163*a*.

86

אל יאמר‎ .אַל‎ with the jussive, mild protest. See note on 17¹³.

Verse 9. סריס‎. Strictly 'eunuch', but used generally for 'court official'.

מהרה‎. 2 m. s. imperat. (with emphatic *he*, DG 84, WL 86) piel of מהר‎ (hasten), here transitive, 'bring quickly'.

Verse 10. ומלך‎. *Waw*-copula (-*u* before labial) plus מֶלֶךְ‎ (king).

ויהושפט‎. *Waw*-copula plus personal name, *shewa* failing under *yodh* after half-open syllable with -*i*, DG 53, WL 44.

ישבים‎. Masc. pl. act. ptc. qal. of ישב‎ (sit).

כסאו‎. 3 m. s. suffix plus masc. noun כִּסֵּא‎ (throne), *dagesh* (due to an original *resh*, cf. Aramaic, Arabic) failing in *samech*-with-*shewa*, DG 33, WL 20.

מלבשים‎. Masc. pl. ptc. pual of לָבֵשׁ‎ (be clothed), followed by accus. of what is worn, WL 108, §75*c*; GK 117*y*.

בגרן‎. Prep. *beth* plus masc. noun גֹּרֶן‎ (threshing floor). A dittograph of previous word. LXX has ἔνοπλοι for both words. AV has 'in a void place', RV 'in an open place', following Vulgate here, and Lucian and LXX in the parallel verse in Chronicles. Here Lucian has 'in the road'. None of these is a justifiable translation of the Hebrew.

Verse 11. קרני. Cstr. pl. of fem. noun קֶרֶן (horn). It is usual for the instrument and its material to be in apposition (GK 131*d*, 127*h*), but here we have a construct construction. בַּרְזֶל (with last vowel short) is 'iron'.

תנגח. 2 m. s. impf. piel of נגח (push, thrust, gore).

כלתם. Inf. cstr. piel of כלה (finish, destroy) plus 3 m. pl. suffix.

Verse 12. נבאים. Masc. pl. ptc. niphal of נבא (prophesy).

והצלח. *Waw*-copula plus 2 m. s. imperat. hiphil of צלח (prosper).

ונתן. Strong-*waw* plus 3 m. s. pf. qal of נתן ('and the LORD will give'), object understood, presumably Ramoth Gilead.

Verse 13. הלך. Translate as pluperfect.

לקרא. Prep. *lamedh* plus inf. cstr. qal of קרא I (call),

יהי. 3 m. s. impf. (apocopated, jussive) qal of היה. 'let (thy word) be', DG 147, WL 145.

דבריך. The Qere is the singular 'thy word'.

Verse 14. חי יהוה. Oath: see note on 17[1]. Normally the positive oath is introduced by אם לא. The use of כי is rare, DS 165, GK 149*a*.

Verse 15. הנלך. Interrogative-*he* plus 1 pl. impf. qal of הלך (go).

אִם־נֶחְדַּל. אִם introduces the second question (here alternative), followed by 1 pl. impf. qal of חדל (refrain), *qamets* for *pathach* in pause.

וְהִצְלַח. See note on verse 12.

Verse 16. עַד־כַּמָּה. Lit. 'to like the what?', i.e. 'how many?'

פְּעָמִים. See note on 17²¹.

מַשְׁבִּעֶךָ. Masc. s. ptc. hiphil of שבע (swear) plus 2 m. s. suffix, with tone retracted with *athnach*, so that vocal *shewa* becomes *seghol*. The substance of the oath is introduced in the form of indirect speech, and by אֲשֶׁר (not כִּי), more frequent in later books, DS 196, GK 157c.

Verse 17. רָאִיתִי. LXX and Lucian introduce the true oracle with לָכֵן, i.e. 'well, then (if you demand the truth)'.

נְפֹצִים. Masc. pl. ptc. niphal of פוּץ (be scattered).

אֶל. We would expect here the prep. עַל (upon). So Targum, Syriac and the parallel in Chronicles.

הֶהָרִים. Article plus plural of הַר (mountain).

כַּצֹּאן. Prep. *kaph* (like) plus article (DS 26, GK 126d) plus צֹאן (sheep).

רֹעֶה. Masc. s. act. ptc. qal of רעה (pasture), acting as noun meaning 'shepherd'.

אֲדֹנִים. Plural (of majesty, DS 18, GK 124i) of אָדֹן (lord).

89

לאלה. Prep. *lamedh* plus article plus demonstrative pronoun plural. 'No master have these: let them return (3 m. pl. impf. qal of שׁוּב) each man to his house in peace'.

Verse 18. A clear case of כי אם after a negative, and meaning 'except'.

Verse 19. מימינו. Prep. *min* plus יָמִין (right) plus 3 m. s. suffix.

ומשמאלו. *Waw*-copula (-*u* before labial) plus *min* plus שׁמאל (left) plus 3 m. s. suffix.

Verse 20. יפתה. 3 m. s. impf. piel of פתה (be simple): in piel 'entice'.

ויעל. Weak-*waw* (*iva*-clause: 'that he may go up') plus 3 m. s. impf. (apoc., jussive) qal of עלה (go up); followed by similar form נפל (fall).

ויאמר זה....זה, 'and this one said thus, and that one saying thus', DG 48.

Verse 21. הרוח, 'the spirit', i.e. the particular spirit who did go. We should use the indefinite 'a' here, DS 26, GK 126*d*.

ויעמד. See note on 19¹³.

אפתנו. 1 s. impf. piel of פתה (entice) plus *nun-energicum* (DG 110, WL 150) plus 3 m. s. suffix.

Verse 22. אצא. 1 s. impf. qal of יצא (go out, forth).

והייתי. Strong-*waw* plus 1 s. pf. qal of היה (be).

רוח שקר, 'spirit of falsehood'.

בפי. Prep. *beth* plus cstr. sing. of masc. noun פֶּה (mouth), DG 153, WL 185.

תפתה. 2 m. s. impf. piel of פתה (entice).

תוכל. 2 m. s. impf. qal of יָכֹל (be able), DG 129, WL 138, GK 69*r*, with *qamets* for *pathach* in pause with *zaqeph-qaton*.

צא. See note on 19[11].

ועשה. *Waw*-copula plus 2 m. s. imperat. qal of עשה (do).

Verse 24. ויגש. See note on 18[21].

ויכה. Strong-*waw* plus 3 m. s. impf. (not apocopated) hiphil of נכה (smite), GK 75*t*.

הלחי. Article plus masc. noun לְחִי (cheek); tone moved to previous syllable, and *seghol* for vocal *shewa* in pause with *athnach*, DG 41, WL 117, GK 29*n*.

זה is enclitic, to emphasise the interrogative אֵי, DS 5, GK 136*c*. When this interrogative is by itself or with another adverb, the form is אֵי, but *pathach* is found when suffixes are added, BDB 32a. 'Where, then?' The syntax here is curious, this being the only place where אי־זה is found without a noun. The parallel in Chronicles supplies הַדֶּרֶךְ, which is correct syntax.

מאתי. Prep. *min* plus prep. אֵת (with) plus 1 s. suffix.

לדבר. Prep. *lamedh* plus inf. cstr. piel of דבר (speak).

אותך. Particle אֵת (denoting definite accusative) plus 2 m. s. suffix. Normally אוֹתְךָ, but here with tone retracted in pause with *silluq*, DG 75 and especially WL 49. The reading ought really to be אִתָּךְ in pause for אִתְּךָ, from prep. אֵת (with), DG 142, WL 149.

Verse 25. הנך. Demonstrative particle הִנֵּה (behold) plus 2 m. s. suffix, DG 142, WL 110f, GK 100*o* and 147*b*. 'Behold you will be seeing (act. ptc. qal) in that day, when . . .', with אשר as true relative.

תבא. 2 m. s. impf. qal of בּוֹא (come).

חדר. Masc. noun (room).

להחבה. Prep. *lamedh* (to) plus inf. cstr. niphal of חבא (hide). The form is *lamedh-he* but with *lamedh-aleph* vowels, GK 75*pp*.

Verse 26. קח. 2 m. s. imperat. qal of לקח (take), DG 213, WL 255.

והשיבהו. *Waw*-copula plus 2 m. s. imperat. hiphil (הָשֵׁב) of שׁוּב (return) plus 3 m. s. suffix.

שׂר. Cstr. sing. (same form) of שַׂר (prince, captain).

Verse 27. ואמרת. Strong-*waw* (tone on last syllable) plus 2 m. s. pf. qal of אמר, following an imperative, and so 'and say'.

שׂימו. 2 m. pl. imperat. qal of שִׂים (set, put).

את־זה. Masc. sing. demonstrative pronoun (preceded by accus. את), used here contemptuously (cf. Latin *iste*), DS 4, GK 136*b*, and examples in Burney.

הכלא. Article plus masc. noun כֶּלֶא (confinement, restraint).

והאכילהו. *Waw*-copula plus 2 m. pl. imperat. hiphil of אכל (eat) plus 3 m. s. suffix. Hiphil-*i* returns with suffixes.

לחץ. In each case this word ('oppression') is in apposition to the previous noun, DS 41, GK 131*c*.

באי. Inf. cstr. qal of בוא (come) plus 1 sinf. suffix.

Verse 28. שׁוב. Inf. absolute qal of שׁוב (return), placed before finite form of same verb (2 m. s. impf. qal) for emphasis, DG 77, WL 101, DS 117, GK 113*n*.

ויאמר ..., 'and he said, Hear ye, O peoples, all of them'. Not in LXX and Lucian. Gloss from Micah 1[2] to identify this prophet with Micah of Moresheth-gath.

כלם. Noun כֹּל (all) plus 3 m. pl. suffix. Double-*ayin* root, with long-*o* sharpening to short-*u* before doubled letter, cf. hophal of *pe-nun* verbs, DG 113, WL 130.

Verse 29. ויעל. See note on 18[43]: here 'advance (to battle)'.

Verse 30. התחפש ובא. These two forms might be 2 m. s. imperatives, but it is best to regard them as inf. absolutes, representing the action itself forcibly presented, DS 121, GK 113*z*. Here it is the 1 person impf. which is intended, cf. Syriac, Targum and LXX (B, L)

συνκαλύφομαι καὶ ἐισελεύσομαι. In any case the 'thou'
of the next clause makes it clear that Ahab is here
speaking of himself. The first form is inf. abs. hithpael
of חפש (in qal 'search', but in hithpael 'make oneself
to be searched for', i.e. 'disguise'). It is followed by
waw-copula (*qamets* before tone in a pair, DG 53,
WL 45) plus inf. abs. qal of בּוֹא (come, enter).

לבש. 2 m. s. imperat. qal of לָבַשׁ or לָבֵשׁ (put on, be
clothed): takes direct object of what is put on, GK
117*y*.

בגדיך. 2 m. s. suffix to plural of masc. noun בֶּגֶד
(garment).

ויתחפש. Strong-*waw* plus 3 m. s. impf. hithpael of
חפש, 'and he disguised himself'.

Verse 31. 'Now the Syrian king *had* commanded . . .',
DS 59, DT 22.

שָׂרֵי. Cstr. pl. of שַׂר (captain). The *qamets* is firm
because root is double-*ayin*.

הרכב. Article plus collective noun 'chariotry'. The
word is occasionally used of a single chariot, but the
normal word for a single chariot is מֶרְכָּבָה.

לא with imperfect is a strong prohibition: see note
on 17[13].

תלחמו. 2 m. pl. impf. niphal of לחם (fight).

את־. Preposition 'with'.

94

כי אם 'except' after a negative, DG 168, WL 111, DS 203, GK 163a.

לבדו. See note on 18⁶.

Verse 32. כראות. See note on 18¹⁷.

אַךְ. 'Nay, but'. Cf. אַף, which is 'yes, and'.

ויסרו. Strong-*waw* plus 3 m. pl. impf. qal of סור (turn aside). LXX and Lucian agree with the parallel in Chronicles and read וַיָּסֹבּוּ 'and they surrounded him', probably correctly.

להלחם. Prep. *lamedh* plus inf. cstr. niphal of לחם (fight).

ויזעק. Strong-*waw* plus 3 m. s. impf. qal of זעק (cry out).

Verse 34. משך, drag along, but 'draw' of a bow, followed by *beth* (instrumentative) plus article plus קֶשֶׁת (bow).

בתמו. Prep. *beth* (in) plus 3 m. s. suffix to sing. of masc. noun תֹּם (integrity): a double-*ayin* root, hence *dagesh* in *mem*. 'At a venture' is good. He took no particular aim, and the theory is that the arrow was supernaturally guided.

ויכה. See note on verse 24.

בין הדבקים . . . . Lit. 'between the attachments and between the breast armour'. דֶּבֶק apparently means 'joint, soldering' (Isa. 41⁷). Possibly the arrow pierced Ahab between the rigid breast-armour and the loose attachments (loose to facilitate movement) which covered the abdomen.

95

לרכבו. Prep. *lamedh* plus רַכָּב (charioteer) plus 3 m. s. suffix. The form קַטָּל denotes occupation, GK 84^{a}b.

הפך. 2 m. s. imperat. qal of הפך 'turn' the hand, and so the chariot-horse.

ידך. This is the singular. Some texts have the plural.

והוציאני. *Waw*-copula plus 2 m. s. imperat. hiphil (הוֹצֵא) of יצא (go out) plus 1 s. suffix. The hiphil-*i* returns with suffixes.

המחנה. The word usually means 'army in camp', but here it apparently means an army 'even while in the thick of the fight', cf. BDB 334a (end).

החליתי. 1 s. pf. hophal of חלה (be ill): RV, 'for I am sore wounded'.

Verse 35. ותעלה. Strong-*waw* plus 3 f. s. impf. (not apocopated) qal of עלה (go up), here of increased intensity.

מעמד. Pual participle of עמד (stand). The use of the participle with the verb 'to be' is precursor of the composite tenses of later Hebrew. It expresses duration of action, 'was propped up', DS 136 (Rem 2), DT 170. Chronicles has hiphil ptc., 'kept himself standing'.

נכח. Properly noun (front), but used always as adverb or (as here) preposition. LXX and Lucian say 'from morning to evening'; Chronicles 'to evening'.

וימת בערב 'and he died in the evening (at dusk)' should probably be transferred to the end of the verse, cf. LXX and Lucian.

וַיִּצֶק. Strong-*waw* plus 3 m. s. impf. qal of יצק (pour out). Some texts have *tsere* under the *yodh*, but *chireq* has the stronger tradition. The impf. qal of this verb is usually a transitive יִצֶק, but here we have an intransitive form. The pointing of the verb varies, GK 69*f*, 71.

מכה. Fem. noun 'wound, blow'.

Verse 36. 'and the cry '(Versions הָרֹנֶה, the herald') passed through the army at sunset . . .'

כבא. Prep. *kaph* plus inf. cstr. qal of בוא (come). Here with שמש (sun) as entering his bed-chamber and so 'set'.

Verse 37. LXX ends the previous verse with 'for the king is dead', and begins this verse with the plural ויבאו 'and they came to Samaria'.

ויקברו. Strong-*waw* plus 3 m. pl. impf. qal of קבר (bury).

Verse 38. וישטף. Strong-*waw* plus 3 m. s. impf. qal of שטף (wash out, swill out). Impersonal construction, GK 114*d*: cf. French *on* and German *man*.

ברכת. Cstr. sing. of fem. noun בְּרֵכָה (pool).

וילקו. Strong-*waw* plus 3 m. pl. impf. qal of לקק (lick up).

והזנות רחצו, 'and the harlots bathed (there)'. LXX and Lucian add 'in the (his) blood'. Vulgate, Syriac and Targum have no reference to harlots, but read 'and they washed the armour', taking זונה wrongly to be זֵין, Aramaic and Rabbinic Hebrew for 'armour'. But רחץ is used only of washing the body; wash clothes is כבס.

דבר. Pausal from (*tsere* for *seghol*) of דְּבֶּר with *seghol*. See note on 21².

Verse 39. השן. Article plus fem. noun שֵׁן (tooth, ivory). Ahab was a great builder.

Verse 42. במלכו. Prep. *beth* plus inf. cstr. qal (short-*o* in half-open syllable) of מלך (become king) plus 3 m. s. suffix.

אמו. 3 m. s. suffix plus sing. of אֵם (mother), double-*ayin* root, DG 140 (like חֵץ), WL 190 (like לֵב).

בת. Cstr. sing. of בַּת (daughter), DG 153, WL 186.

Verse 43. וילך. See note on 17⁵.

ממנו. Prep. *min* plus 3 m. s. suffix, DG 53, WL 110f.

Verse 44. הבמות. Article plus plural of fem. noun בָּמָה (high place).

סרו. 3 pl. pf. qal of סור (turn aside). The Versions assume הֵסִיר (3 m. s. pf. hiphil), 'he did not remove'.

מזבחים. Masc. pl. of piel ptc. of זבח (sacrifice). Here probably 'slaughter', because the following root קטר means 'sacrifice' in pre-exilic contexts and 'burn incense' in post-exilic contexts.

Verse 45. וישלם. Strong-*waw* plus 3 m. s. impf. (jussive form) hiphil of שלם, denominative verb from שָׁלוֹם (peace); 'made peace'.

Verse 46. וּגְבוּרָתוֹ. *Waw*-copula (-*u* before *shewa*) plus 3 m. s. suffix to sing. of fem. noun גְּבוּרָה (might).

נִלְחַם. 3 m. s. pf. niphal of לחם (fight), with *qamets* for *pathach* in pause with *athnach*.

כְּתוּבִים. Masc. pl. of pass. ptc. qal of כתב (write).

Verse 47. The קָדֵשׁ was a male temple prostitute.

נִשְׁאַר. 3 m. s. pf. niphal of שאר (leave over).

בִּימֵי. Prep. *beth* plus יְמֵי, cstr. pl. of יוֹם (day), DG 153, WL 186. The *shewa* fails under *yodh* after half-open syllable with *chireq*, DG 51, WL 43.

אָבִיו. 3 m. s. suffix plus sing. אָב (father), DG 153, WL 186.

בִּעֵר. 3 m. s. pf. piel of בער (burn out, extirpate).

Verse 48. RV 'and there was no king in Edom; a deputy was king', but no one likes it, and the Versions do not help materially. Targum, almost agrees: 'and there was no king in Edom appointed; a general was king', apparently repeating נצב. Stade suggested: 'and there was no king in Edom; but the deputy of נְצִיב king Jehoshat made . . .'

Verse 49. עָשָׂר. Follow the Qere עָשָׂה (made).

אֳנִיּוֹת. Cstr. pl. of אֳנִיָּה (ship). A 'ship of Tarshish' was a large 'ocean-going' ship.

לָלֶכֶת. Prep. *lamedh* (*gamets* before an inf. coustr.) plus inf. cstr. qal (לֶכֶת) of הלך (go).

אוֹפִירָה. *He-locale* (DG 61f, WL 55 and 211) plus place-name.

99

הלך. 3 m. s. pf. qal of הלך (go), with *qamets* for *pathach* in pause with *athnach*.

נשברה. The Kethib is נִשְׁבְּרָה, 3 f. s. pf. niphal of שבר (break), as if of the fleet as a whole. The Qere is the plural.

Verse 50. ילכו. 3 m. pl. impf. (jussive) qal of הלך, 'let my servants go with your servants'.

באניות. Prep. *beth* plus article plus pl. of אֳנִיָּה (ship).

Verse 51. וישכב. See note on 19⁵.

אבתיו. 3 m. s. suffix to plural of אָב (father), DG 153, WL 185.

ויקבר. Strong-*waw* plus 3 m. s. impf. niphal of קבר (bury).

Verse 52. שנתים. Dual of fem. noun שָׁנָה (year), with *qamets* for *pathach* in pause with *silluq*.

Verse 53. ויעש. See note on 17⁵.

החטיא. 3 m. s. pf. hiphil of חטא (sin).

Verse 54. ויעבד. Strong-*waw* plus 3 m. s. impf. qal of עבד (serve, worship).

וישתחוה. Strong-*waw* plus 3 m. s. impf. hithpalel of שחה (bow down). See DG 145, WL 145, GK 75*kk* for an explanation of this unusual form, here not apocopated.

ויכעס. Strong-*waw* plus 3 m. s. impf. (jussive form) hiphil of כעס (be jealous).

VOCABULARY

אָב n.m.—father

אבה v.—be willing

אֶבֶן n.f.—stone

אֲדָמָה n.f.—ground

אָדוֹן n.m.—lord

אַדֶּרֶת n.f.—cloak

אוּלַי adv.—perhaps

אָז adv.—then

אֶחָד, אַחַד—one (m)

אַחַר prep.—after

אַחֲרוֹן adj.—last

אַחֲרֵי prep.—after

אֲחֹרַנִּית adv.—backwards

אַט adj.—gently

אֹיֵב n.m.—enemy

אַיִן adv.—no

אִישׁ n.m.—man

אַךְ adv.—but

אֲכִילָה n.f.—food

אכל v.—eat

אֶל prep.—to

אֵלֶּה pron.—these

אֱלֹהִים n.m.—God

אַלְמָנָה n.f.—widow

אֶלֶף n.m.—thousand

אֵם n.f.—mother

אִם conj.—if

אמר v.—say

אֱמֶת n.f.—truth

אֲנַחְנוּ pron.—we

אֲנִי pron.—I

אֳנִיָּה n.f.—ship

אָנֹכִי pron.—I

אסר v.—bind

אֵצֶל prep.—beside

אַרְבַּע—four

אַרְבָּעִים—forty

אֶרֶץ n.f.—earth, land

אֵשׁ n.f.—fire

אִשָּׁה n.f.—woman

אֲשֶׁר—relative

אֵת prep.—with

אֵת (def. acc. follows)

אַתָּה pron.—thou (m)

אַתֶּם pron.—ye (m)

ב

בֶּגֶד n.m.—garment
בְּהֵמָה n.f.—cattle
בוא v.—come
בחר v.—choose
בֵּין prep.—between
בַּיִת n.m.—house
בָּמָה n.f.—hill-shrine
בֵּן n.m.—son
בנה v.—build
בַּעַל n.m.—Baal
בַּעֲלָה n.f.—mistress
בער v.—burn, consume
בָּקָר n.m.—cattle, ox
בֹּקֶר n.m.—morning
בקש v.—seek
בַּרְזֶל n.m.—iron
בְּרִית n.f.—covenant
ברך v.—bless
בֶּרֶך n.f.—knee
בְּרֵכָה n.f.—pool
בשל v.—boil
בָּשָׂר n.m.—flesh

ג

גְּבוּרָה n.f.—might
גדד v.—cut
גָּדוֹל adj.—great

ד

גהר v.—crouch
גּוֹי n.m.—nation
גור v.—sojourn
גִּלּוּלִים n.m.—idols
גַּם part.—also
גַּן n.m.—garden
גֹּרֶן n.m.—threshing-floor
גֶּשֶׁם n.m.—rain

ד

דָּבֵק n.m.—joint
דבר v.—speak
דָּבָר n.m.—word
דָּם n.m.—blood
דְּמָמָה n.f.—silence
דַּק adj.—crushed
דֶּרֶך n.m.—way, road
דרש v.—seek

ה

הוא pron.—he
הִיא pron.—she
היה v.—be
הֵיכָל n.m.—palace, temple
הלך v.—go
הָמוֹן n.m.—noise, abun-
  dance
הִנֵּה part.—behold

הפך v.—turn back
הר n.m.—mountain
הרג v.—kill
הרס v.—throw down
התל v.—mock

ז

זבח v.—kill, sacrifice
זֶה dem. pro.—this
זָהָב n.m.—gold
זכר v.—remember
זָנָה n.f.—harlot
זָעֵף adj.—vexed
זעק v.—cry out
זָקֵן n.m.—old man, elder
זֶרַע n.m.—seed

ח

חבא v.—hide
חדל v.—cease
חָדָר n.m.—room, chamber
חוּץ n.m.—outside
חָזָק adj.—strong
חטא v.—sin
חַי adj.—living
חיה v.—live
חֵיק n.m.—bosom
חֵל n.m.—rampart
חלה v.—be ill

חֳלִי n.m.—illness
חָלִילָה—*ad profanum*
חלק v.—share, divide
חֲמִשִּׁים—fifty
חָסֵר v.—be lacking
חָפֵץ adj.—delighting in
חפש v.—search, (*hith.*-disguise)
חָצִיר n.m.—grass
חֹר n.m.—noble
חֶרֶב n.f.—sword
חרש v.—cut in, plough
חשה v.—be silent, inactive
חתם v.—seal
חֹתָם n.m.—seal

ט

טוב adj.—good
טַל n.m.—dew

י

יָבֵשׁ v.—be dry
יָד n.f.—hand
ידע v.—know
יוֹם n.m.—day
יטב v.—be good
יָכֹל v.—be able
יֶלֶד n.m.—boy
יָם n.m.—sea

יָמִין n.f.—right hand

יסף v.—add

יַעַן prep., conj.—because, on account of

יצא v.—go out

יצק v.—pour

יקץ v.—awaken

יָרֵא v.—be afraid

ירד v.—go down

יָרָק n.m.—green produce

ירש v.—take possession of

יֵשׁ n.m.—being

ישב v.—dwell, sit

ישן v.—be asleep

יָשָׁר adj.—upright

יתר v.—remain over

יֶתֶר n.m.—remainder

כ

כַּד n.f.—jar

כֹּה adv.—thus

כוּל v.—contain (*pilpel*-nourish)

כֹּחַ n.m.—strength

כִּי־אִם conj.—except

כֹּל (כָּל־) n.m.—all

כֶּלֶא n.m.—imprisonment

כֶּלֶב n.m.—dog

כלה v.—be complete, at an end

כְּלִי n.m.—vessel, utensil

כְּמוֹ prep.—as, like

כֵּן adv.—thus

כנע v.—be humble

כִּסֵּא n.m.—throne

כֶּסֶף n.m.—silver

כעס v.—vex

כַּעַס n.m.—vexation

כַּף n.f.—hollow of hand

כֶּרֶם n.m.—vineyard

כרע v.—bow down

כרת v.—cut, cut off

כתב v.—write

ל

לֹא adv.—net

לֵב n.m.—heart

לְבַד prep.—alone

לבש v.—clothe

לוֹט v.—wrap closely

לְחִי n.m.—jaw

לחך v.—lick

לחם v.—fight

לֶחֶם n.m.—bread

לַחַץ n.m.—distress

לַיְלָה n.m.—night

לין v.—spend the night

לָכֵן adv.—therefore

לִפְנֵי prep.—before
לקח v.—take
לקק v.—lick, lap

מ

מְאֹד adv.—much
מֵאָה —hundred
מְאוּמָה indef. pro.—anything
מאן v.—refuse
מִדְבָּר n.m.—wilderness
מדד v.—measure
מה interrog.—what?
מהר v.—hurry
מות v.—die
מִזְבֵּחַ n.m.—altar
מְחִיר n.m.—price
מַחֲנֶה n.m.—camp
מָחָר n.m.—tomorrow
מִטָּה n.f.—bed
מָטָר n.m.—rain
מִי interrog.—who?
מַיִם n.m.—water
מַכָּה n.f.—wound
מכר v.—sell
מָלֵא v.—be full
מְלֹא n.m.—fulness
מַלְאָךְ n.m.—messenger

מְלוּכָה n.f.—royalty, kingship
מִלְחָמָה n.f.—war, battle
מלט v.—escape, deliver
מלך v.—be king
מֶלֶךְ n.m.—king
מַמְלָכָה n.f.—kingdom
מִנְחָה n.f.—offering
מִסְפָּר n.m.—number
מָעוֹג n.m.—cake
מְעַט n.m.—a little
מַעְיָן n.m.—spring (water)
מְעָרָה n.f.—cave
מצא v.—find
מִצְוָה n.f.—commandment
מָקוֹם n.f.—place
מְרַאֲשׁוֹת n.f.—head-place
מֶרְכָּבָה n.f.—chariot
משׁח v.—anoint
משׁך v.—draw (bow)
מִשְׁפָּט n.m.—custom
מָתַי adv.—when?
מָתְנַיִם n.m.—loins

נ

נָא—(particle of entreaty)
נבא v.—prophesy
נבט v.—(hiph) look

נָבִיא n.m.—prophet

נגד v.—(hiph) tell

נֶגֶד prep.—in front of

נגח v.—push, gore

נגע v.—touch

נגש v.—draw near

נוח v.—leave, rest

נַחַל n.m.—wady, torrent

נַחֲלָה n.f.—inheritance

נכה v.—(hiph) smite

נֹכַח prep.—facing

נכר v.—recognise

נַעַר n.m.—youth, young man

נְעָרִים n.m.—youth (time)

נפל v.—fall

נֶפֶשׁ n.f.—life, breath-soul

נִצָּב n.m.—deputy

נשא v.—lift up

נְשָׁמָה n.f.—breath

נשק v.—kiss

נתח v.—cut in pieces

נתן v.—give

נתר v.—disjoint, cut in joints

ס

סְאָה n.f.—seah (10 qts.)

סבב v.—go round

סָבִיב adj.—round

סוּס n.m.—horse

סור v.—turn aside

סות v.—incite

סֶלַע n.m.—crag

סלק v.—stone (throw)

סְעִפָּה n.f.—division

סֵפֶר n.m.—missive, book

סַר adj.—sullen

סָרִיס n.m.—eunuch

סתר v.—cover, hide

ע

עָב n.m. & f.—cloud

עבד v.—serve, worship

עֶבֶד n.m.—servant, slave

עבר v.—cross over

עֻגָה n.f.—cake

עַד prep.—to

עוֹד adv.—yet, still

עוד v.—bear witness

עָוֹן n.m.—iniquity

עוֹף n.m.—birds

עזב v.—forsake

עַיִן n.f.—eye

עִיר n.f.—city

עכר v.—trouble

עלה v.—go up

עֹלָה n.f.—burnt offering

עֲלִיָה n.f.—upper room

עַם n.m.—people

עִם prep.—with

עמד v.—stand

ענה v.—answer

עָפָר n.m.—dust

עֵץ n.m.—tree

עצר v.—restrain

עֶרֶב n.m.—evening

עֹרֵב n.m.—raven

ערך v.—arrange

עשׂה v.—do

עָשָׂר—ten

עֵת n.f.—time

עַתָּה adv.—now

פ

פֶּה n.m.—mouth

פֹּה adv.—here

פוץ v.—be scattered

פנה v.—turn

פָּנִים n.m.—face

פסח v.—limp

פַּעַם n.m.—blow, time

פַּר n.m.—ox

פֶּרֶד n.m.—mule

פרק v.—tear apart

פַּת n.f.—fragment

פתה v.—deceive

פֶּתַח n.m.—opening

צ

צֹאן n.f.—sheep

צָבָא n.m.—host

צָהֳרַיִם n.m.—noonday

צוה v.—command

צוֹם n.m.—fast

צלח v.—prosper

צֶמֶד n.m.—pair

צַפַּחַת n.f.—jar

ק

קבץ v.—gather

קבר v.—bury

קֵדְמָה adv.—eastwards

קדר v.—be dark

קָדֵשׁ n.m.—male prostitute

קוֹל n.m.—voice

קום v.—arise

קָטוֹן adj.—little

קָטָן adj.—little

קטר v.—make smoke, sacrifice

קִיר n.m.—wall

קֶמַח n.m.—flour

קנא v.—be jealous, zealous

קֵץ n.m.—end

קרא I, v.—call

קרא II, v.—meet

קֶרֶב n.m.—inward part

107

קָרוֹב adj.—near

קֶרֶן n.f.—horn

קרע v.—tear

קֶשֶׁב n.m.—attentiveness

קשׁשׁ v.—gather stubble

קֶשֶׁת n.f.—bow

ר

ראה v.—see

רֹאשׁ n.m.—head, top

רִאשׁוֹן adj.—first

רַב adj.—many

רוּחַ n.f.—wind, spirit

רוּץ v.—run

רחץ v.—bathe

רכב v.—ride

רַכָּב n.m.—charioteer

רֶכֶב n.m.—chariotry

רֹמַח n.m.—lance, lancet

רִנָּה n.f.—ringing cry

רַע n.m.—evil

רָעָב n.m.—famine

רָעָה n.f.—evil

רֹעֶה n.m.—shepherd

רעע v.—be evil

רַעַשׁ n.m.—earthquake

רפא v.—heal

רצח v.—murder

רִצְפָּה n.f.—glowing stone

רַק adv.—only

רֹתֶם n.m.—broom (plant)

שׂ

שִׂיג n.m.—? moving away

שָׂדֶה n.m.—field, open country

שִׂיחַ n.m.—musing

שׂים v.—set

שְׂמֹאל n.m.—left hand

שָׂנֵא v.—hate

שַׂק n.m.—sackcloth

שַׂר n.m.—captain, prince

שׁ

שׁאל v.—ask

שׁאר v.—remain

שֵׁבֶט n.m.—rod, tribe

שְׁבִיעִית—seventh

שֶׁבַע—seven

שׁבע v.—swear

שׁבר v.—break

שׁוּב v.—return

שׁחה v.—bow down

שׁחט v.—slaughter

שׁטף v.—wash off

שׁכב v.—lie down

שָׁלוֹם n.m.—peace

שׁלח v.—send

שֻׁלְחָן n.m.—table

שְׁלִישִׁית—third

שלך v.—cast

שלם v.—be at peace

שלש v.—do a third time

שָׁלֹש—three

שָׁם adv.—there

שֵׁם n.m.—name

שָׁמַיִם n.m.—heavens

שֶׁמֶן n.m.—oil

שמע v.—hear

שֶׁמֶשׁ n.f.—sun

שֵׁן n.f.—ivory, tooth

שָׁנָה n.f.—year

שנה v.—do a second time

שְׁנֵי ,שְׁנַיִם—two (m)

שֵׁנִית—second

שנס v.—gird up

שַׁעַר n.m.—gate

שפך v.—pour out

שֶׁקֶר n.m.—deception

שִׁרְיֹן n.m.—body armour

שרת v.—minister, serve

שתה v.—drink

שְׁתֵּי ,שְׁתַּיִם—two (f)

שתן v.—urinate

ת

תֹּם n.m.—integrity, inno-
cence

תעב v.—do abominably

תְּעָלָה n.f.—trench

תפש v.—lay hold

תֹּשָׁב n.m.—dweller

תִּשְׁבִּי adj.—Tishbite

תַּחַת prep.—under